Godi + Zidrou

Ducobu

Colour work: Véronique Grobet

Original title: L'élève Ducobu – Les Réponses ou la vie ?

Original edition: © Les Editions du Lombard (Dargaud-Lombard SA), 1999
by Godi & Zidrou
www.lelombard.com

English translation: © 2008 Cinebook Ltd

Translator: Luke Spear
Lettering and text layout: Imadjinn sarl
Printed in Spain by Just Colour Graphic

This edition first published in Great Britain in 2008 by
Cinebook Ltd
56 Beech Avenue
Canterbury, Kent
CT4 7TA
www.cinebook.com

A CIP catalogue record for this book
is available from the British Library

ISBN 978-1-905460-28-1

9th CINEBOOK
The 9th Art Publisher

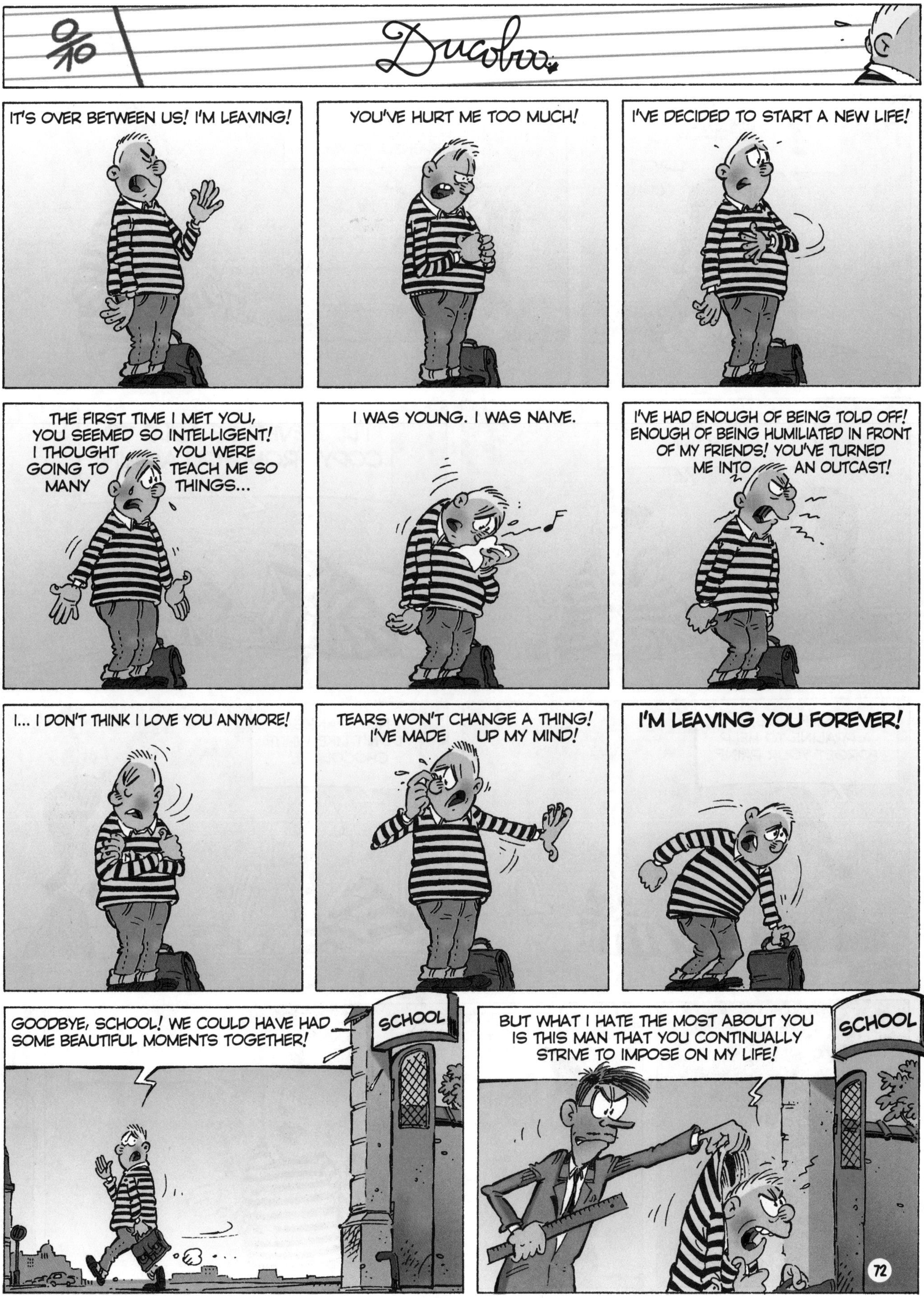
Ducobu
IT'S OVER BETWEEN US! I'M LEAVING!
YOU'VE HURT ME TOO MUCH!
I'VE DECIDED TO START A NEW LIFE!
THE FIRST TIME I MET YOU, YOU SEEMED SO INTELLIGENT! I THOUGHT YOU WERE GOING TO TEACH ME SO MANY THINGS...
I WAS YOUNG. I WAS NAIVE.
I'VE HAD ENOUGH OF BEING TOLD OFF! ENOUGH OF BEING HUMILIATED IN FRONT OF MY FRIENDS! YOU'VE TURNED ME INTO AN OUTCAST!
I... I DON'T THINK I LOVE YOU ANYMORE!
TEARS WON'T CHANGE A THING! I'VE MADE UP MY MIND!
I'M LEAVING YOU FOREVER!
GOODBYE, SCHOOL! WE COULD HAVE HAD SOME BEAUTIFUL MOMENTS TOGETHER!
SCHOOL
BUT WHAT I HATE THE MOST ABOUT YOU IS THIS MAN THAT YOU CONTINUALLY STRIVE TO IMPOSE ON MY LIFE!
SCHOOL
72

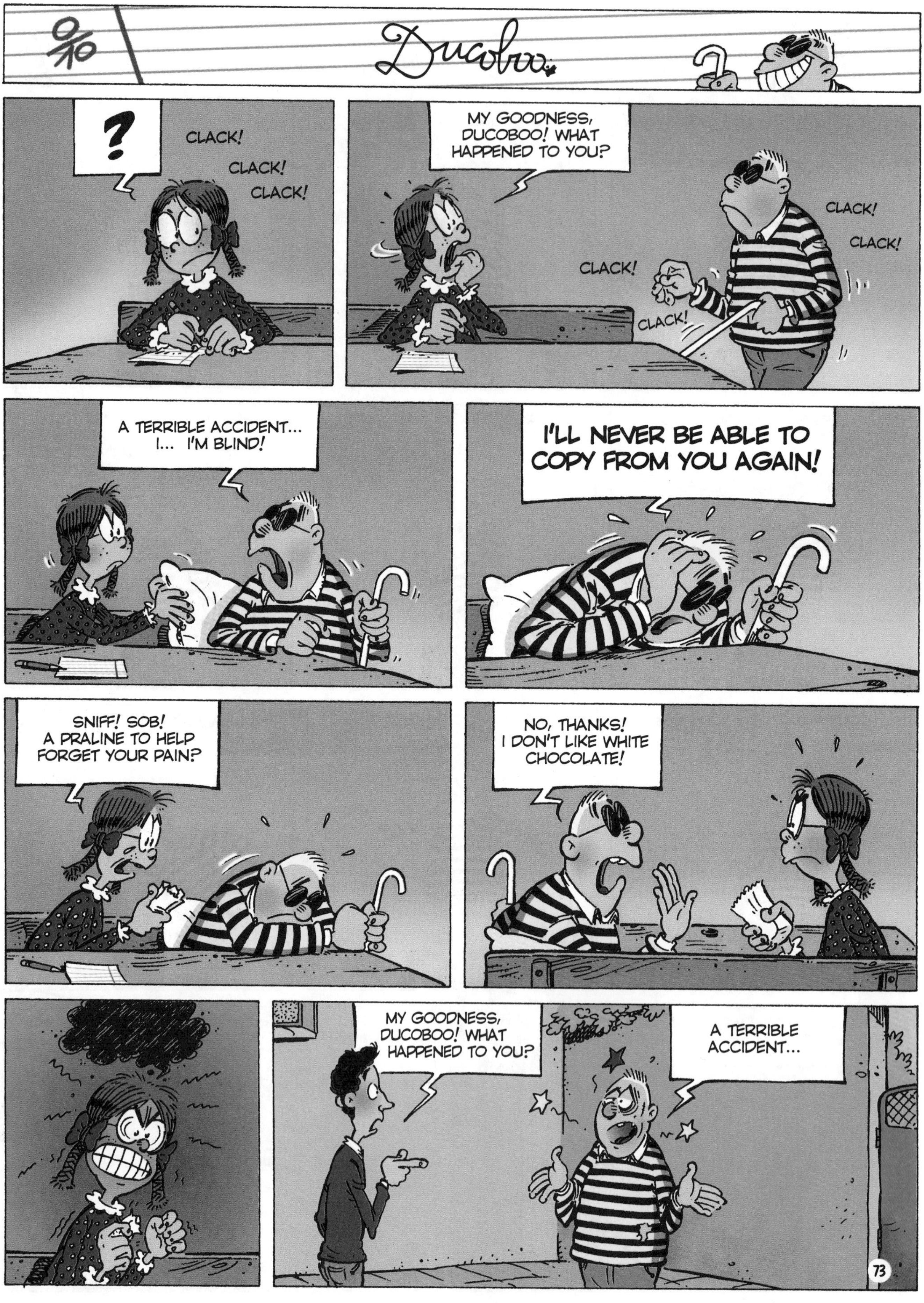
Ducoboo
?
CLACK!
CLACK!
CLACK!
MY GOODNESS, DUCOBOO! WHAT HAPPENED TO YOU?
CLACK!
CLACK!
CLACK!
CLACK!
A TERRIBLE ACCIDENT... I... I'M BLIND!
I'LL NEVER BE ABLE TO COPY FROM YOU AGAIN!
SNIFF! SOB! A PRALINE TO HELP FORGET YOUR PAIN?
NO, THANKS! I DON'T LIKE WHITE CHOCOLATE!
MY GOODNESS, DUCOBOO! WHAT HAPPENED TO YOU?
A TERRIBLE ACCIDENT...
73

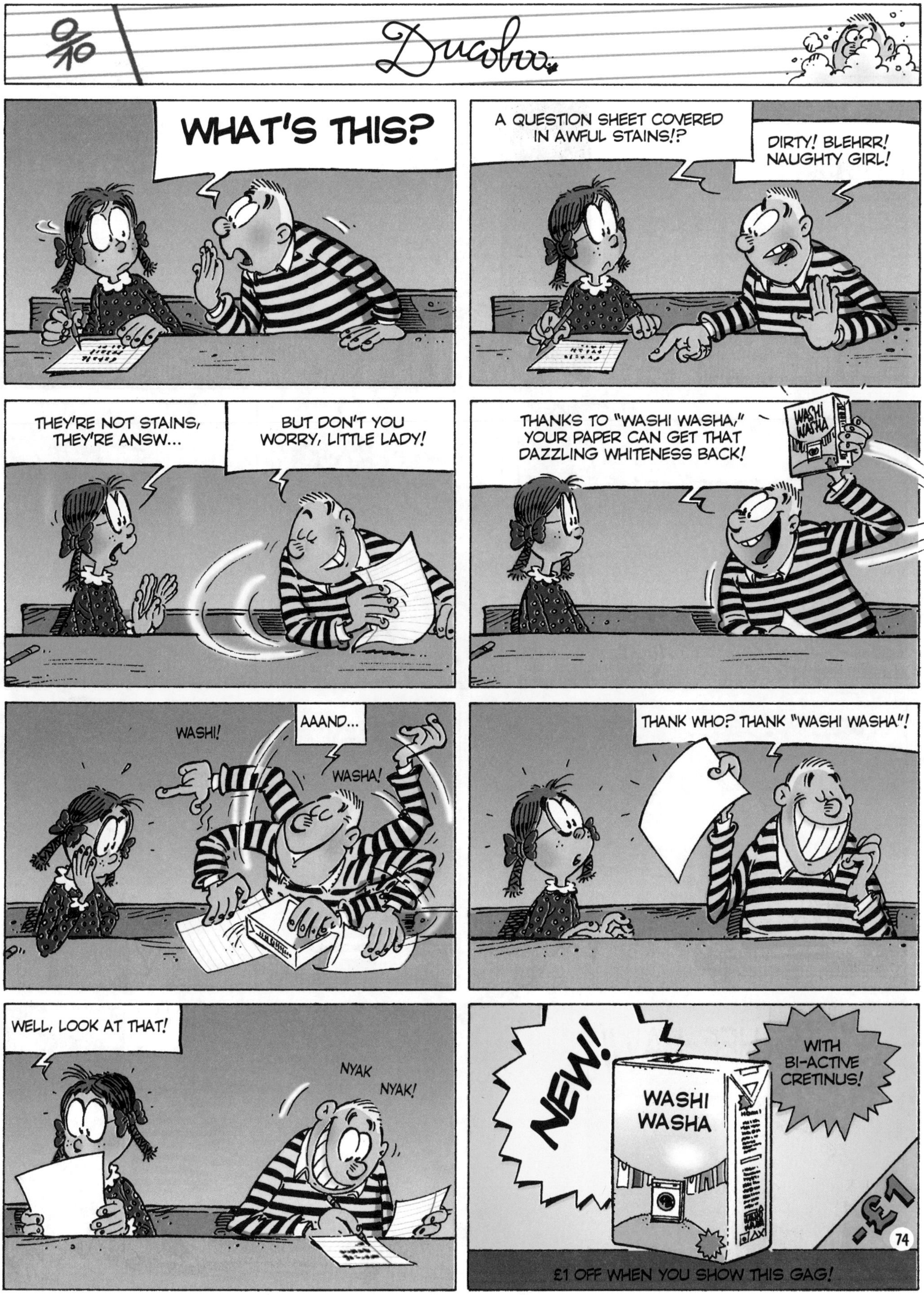

9/10
Ducobu
WHAT'S THIS?
A QUESTION SHEET COVERED IN AWFUL STAINS!?
DIRTY! BLEHRR! NAUGHTY GIRL!
THEY'RE NOT STAINS, THEY'RE ANSW...
BUT DON'T YOU WORRY, LITTLE LADY!
THANKS TO "WASHI WASHA," YOUR PAPER CAN GET THAT DAZZLING WHITENESS BACK!
WASHI WASHA
WASHI!
AAAND...
WASHA!
THANK WHO? THANK "WASHI WASHA"!
WELL, LOOK AT THAT!
NYAK
NYAK!
NEW!
WASHI WASHA
WITH BI-ACTIVE CRETINUS!
-£1
74
£1 OFF WHEN YOU SHOW THIS GAG!

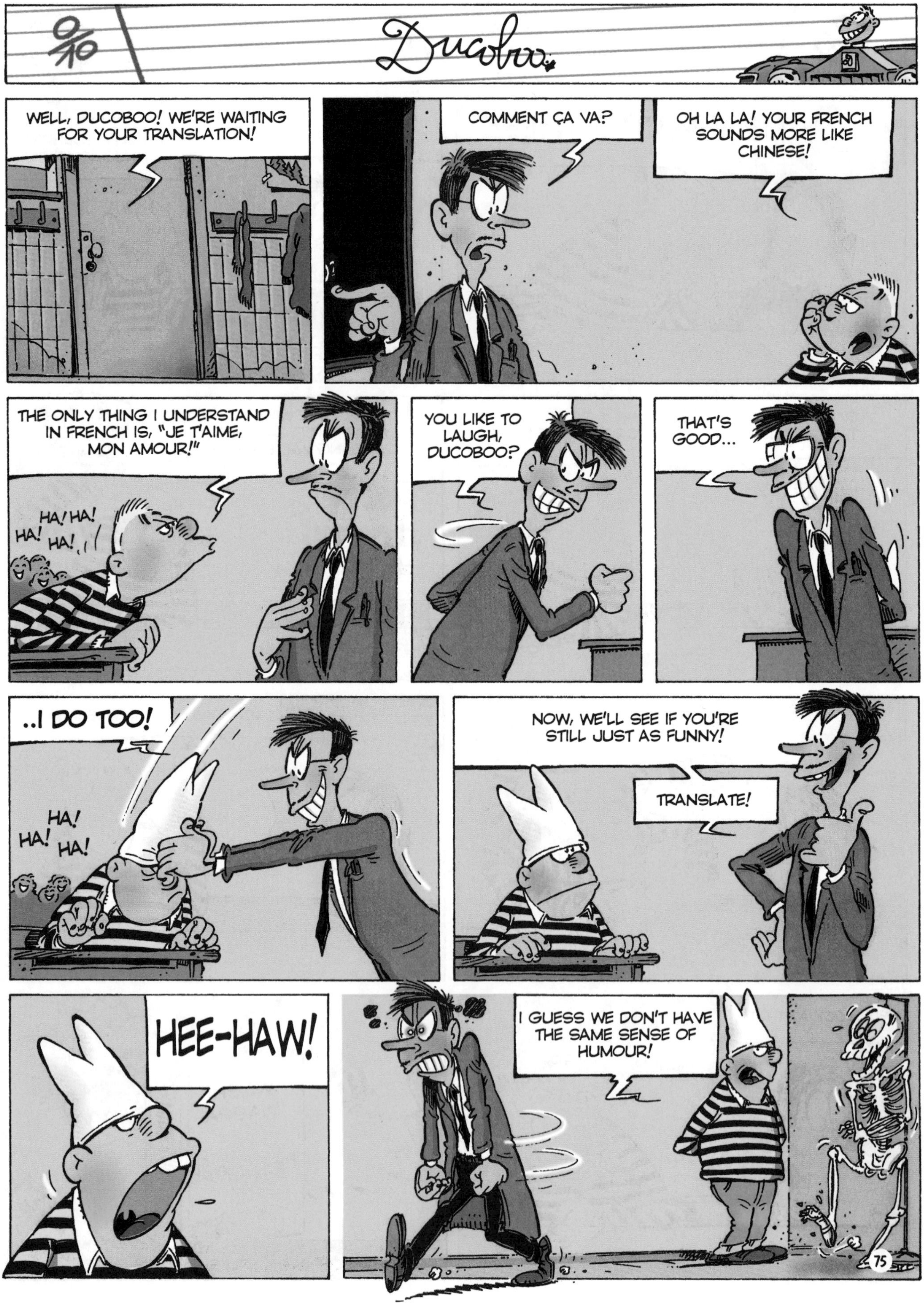
0/10
Ducoboo
WELL, DUCOBOO! WE'RE WAITING FOR YOUR TRANSLATION!
COMMENT ÇA VA?
OH LA LA! YOUR FRENCH SOUNDS MORE LIKE CHINESE!
THE ONLY THING I UNDERSTAND IN FRENCH IS, "JE T'AIME, MON AMOUR!"
HA! HA! HA! HA!
YOU LIKE TO LAUGH, DUCOBOO?
THAT'S GOOD...
..I DO TOO!
HA! HA! HA!
NOW, WE'LL SEE IF YOU'RE STILL JUST AS FUNNY!
TRANSLATE!
HEE-HAW!
I GUESS WE DON'T HAVE THE SAME SENSE OF HUMOUR!
75

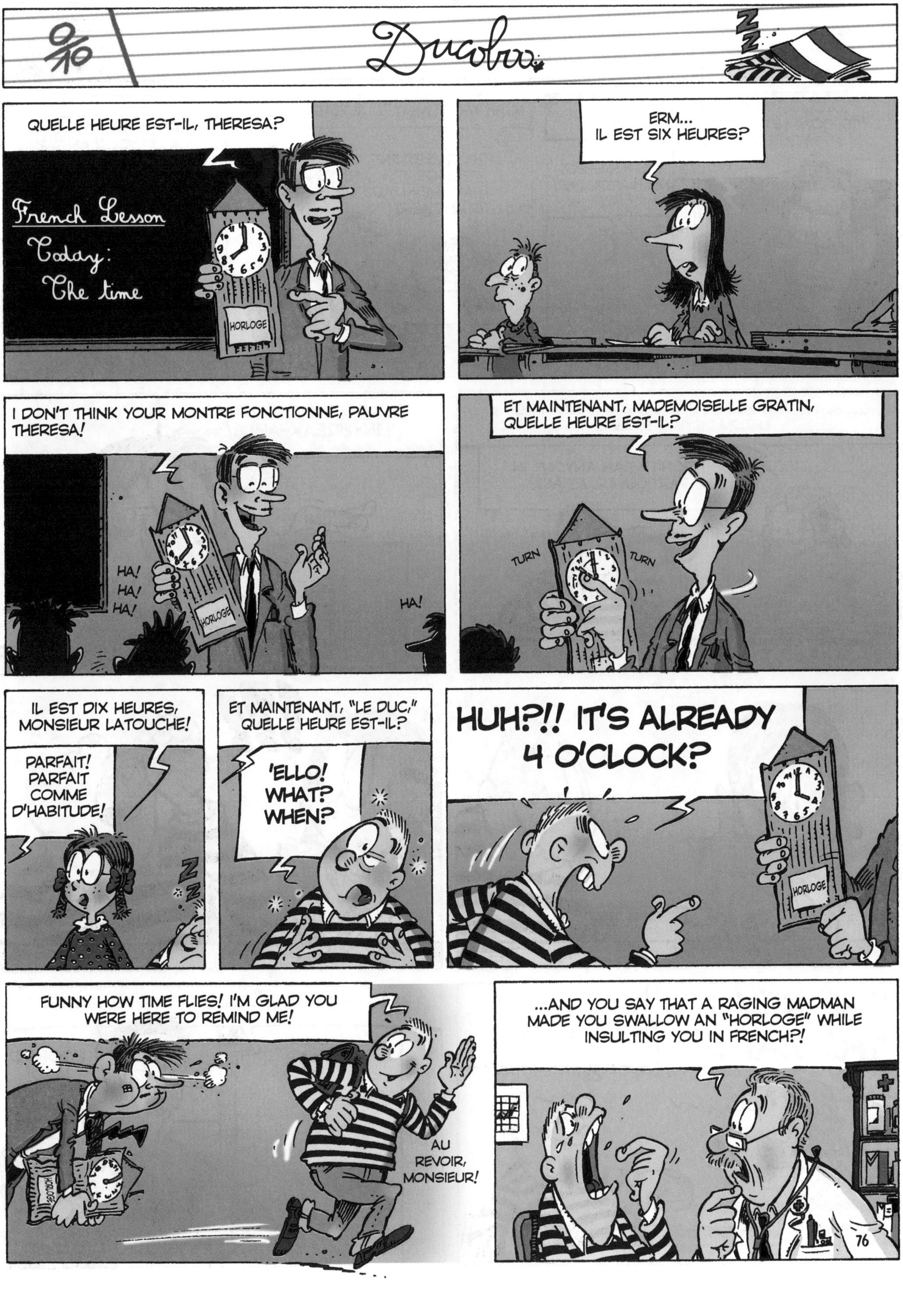
Ducobu
French Lesson
Today:
The time
QUELLE HEURE EST-IL, THERESA?
HORLOGE
ERM... IL EST SIX HEURES?
I DON'T THINK YOUR MONTRE FONCTIONNE, PAUVRE THERESA!
HA! HA! HA!
HA!
ET MAINTENANT, MADEMOISELLE GRATIN, QUELLE HEURE EST-IL?
TURN
TURN
IL EST DIX HEURES, MONSIEUR LATOUCHE!
PARFAIT! PARFAIT COMME D'HABITUDE!
ET MAINTENANT, "LE DUC," QUELLE HEURE EST-IL?
'ELLO! WHAT? WHEN?
HUH?!! IT'S ALREADY 4 O'CLOCK?
FUNNY HOW TIME FLIES! I'M GLAD YOU WERE HERE TO REMIND ME!
AU REVOIR, MONSIEUR!
...AND YOU SAY THAT A RAGING MADMAN MADE YOU SWALLOW AN "HORLOGE" WHILE INSULTING YOU IN FRENCH?!
76

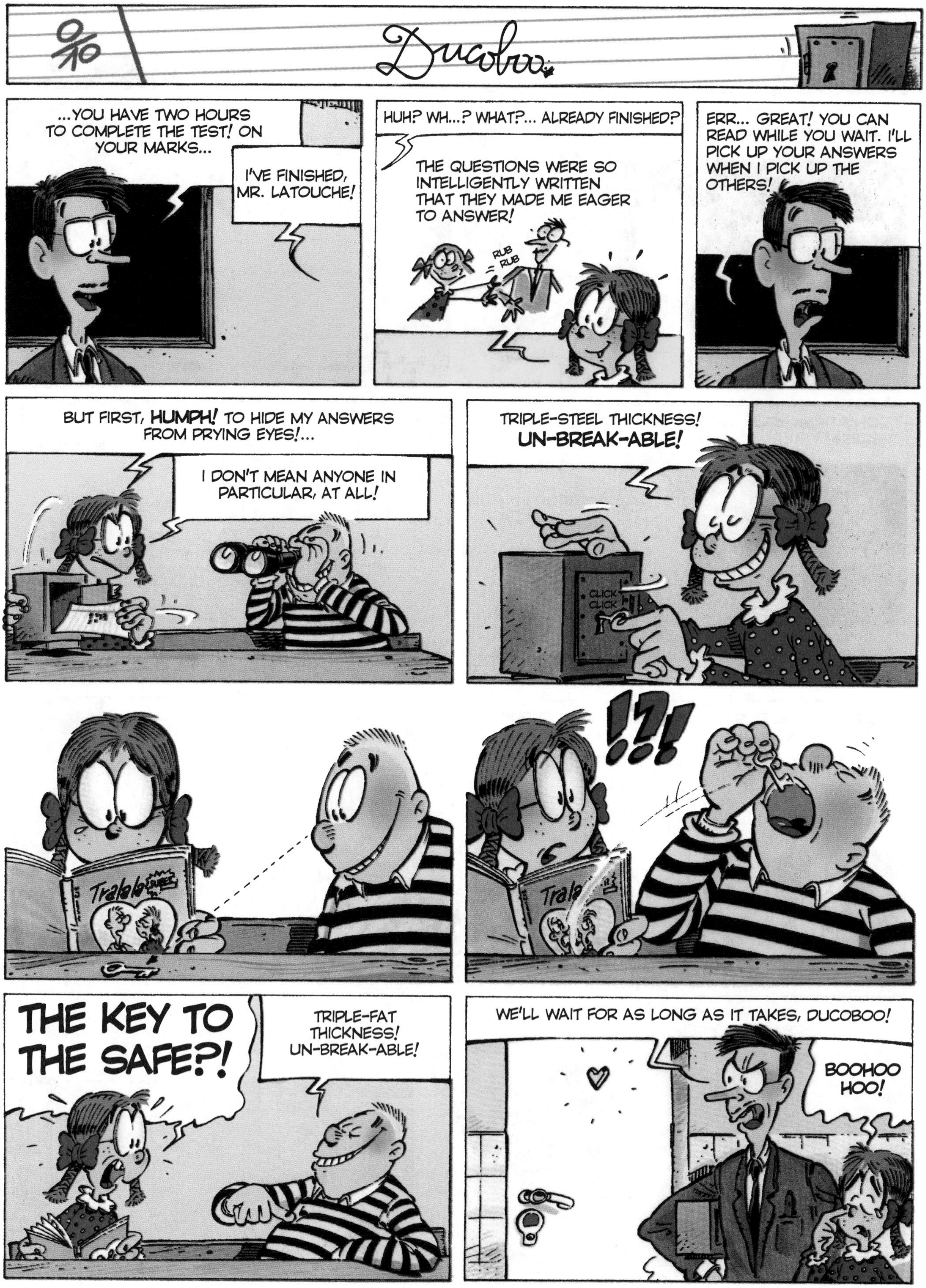
Ducoboo
...YOU HAVE TWO HOURS TO COMPLETE THE TEST! ON YOUR MARKS...
I'VE FINISHED, MR. LATOUCHE!
HUH? WH...? WHAT?... ALREADY FINISHED?
THE QUESTIONS WERE SO INTELLIGENTLY WRITTEN THAT THEY MADE ME EAGER TO ANSWER!
RUB RUB
ERR... GREAT! YOU CAN READ WHILE YOU WAIT. I'LL PICK UP YOUR ANSWERS WHEN I PICK UP THE OTHERS!
BUT FIRST, HUMPH! TO HIDE MY ANSWERS FROM PRYING EYES!...
I DON'T MEAN ANYONE IN PARTICULAR, AT ALL!
TRIPLE-STEEL THICKNESS! UN-BREAK-ABLE!
CLICK CLICK
Tralala
!?!
THE KEY TO THE SAFE?!
TRIPLE-FAT THICKNESS! UN-BREAK-ABLE!
WE'LL WAIT FOR AS LONG AS IT TAKES, DUCOBOO!
BOOHOO HOO!

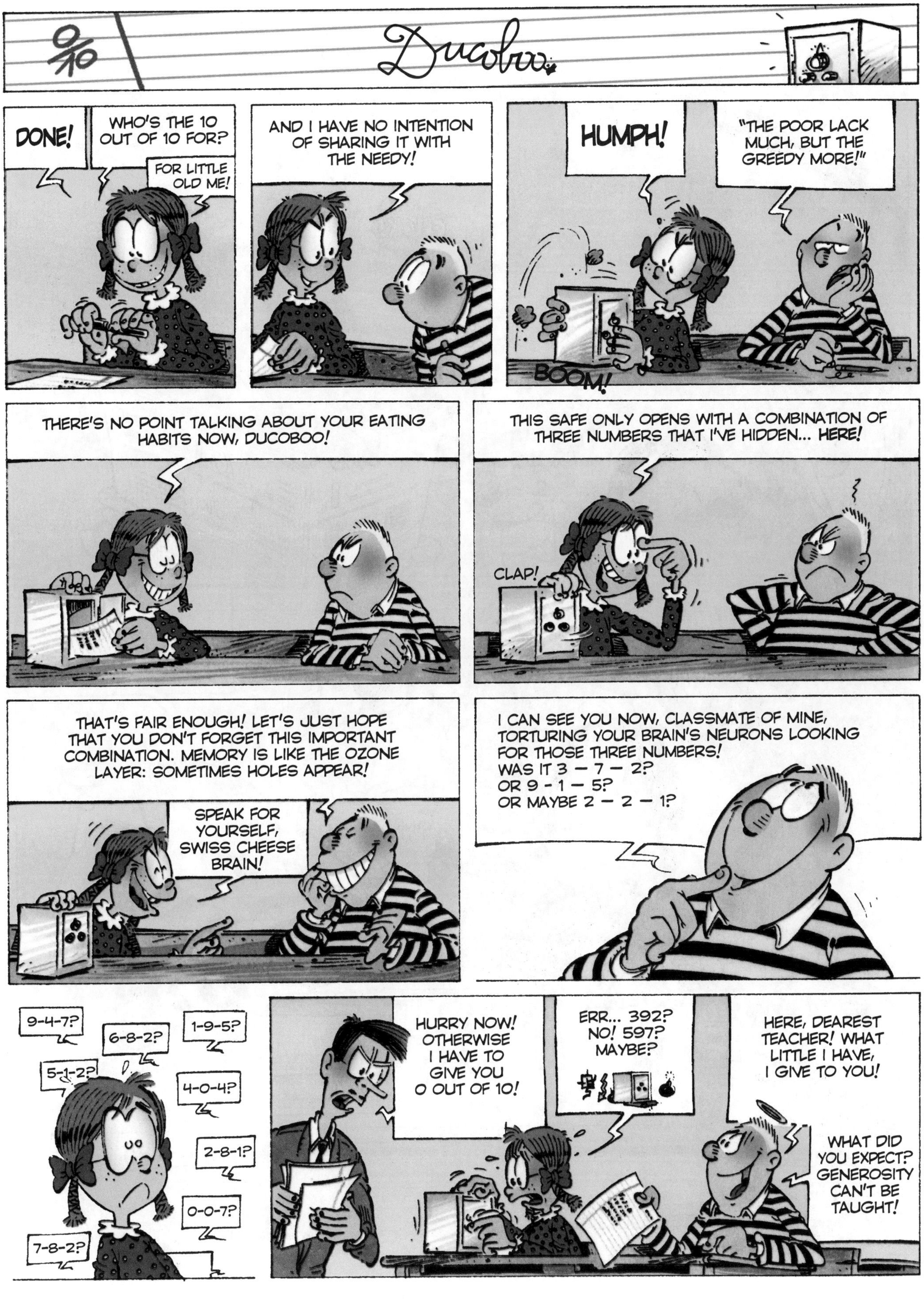
9/10
Ducoboo
DONE!
WHO'S THE 10 OUT OF 10 FOR?
FOR LITTLE OLD ME!
AND I HAVE NO INTENTION OF SHARING IT WITH THE NEEDY!
HUMPH!
"THE POOR LACK MUCH, BUT THE GREEDY MORE!"
BOOM!
THERE'S NO POINT TALKING ABOUT YOUR EATING HABITS NOW, DUCOBOO!
THIS SAFE ONLY OPENS WITH A COMBINATION OF THREE NUMBERS THAT I'VE HIDDEN... HERE!
CLAP!
THAT'S FAIR ENOUGH! LET'S JUST HOPE THAT YOU DON'T FORGET THIS IMPORTANT COMBINATION. MEMORY IS LIKE THE OZONE LAYER: SOMETIMES HOLES APPEAR!
SPEAK FOR YOURSELF, SWISS CHEESE BRAIN!
I CAN SEE YOU NOW, CLASSMATE OF MINE, TORTURING YOUR BRAIN'S NEURONS LOOKING FOR THOSE THREE NUMBERS! WAS IT 3 – 7 – 2? OR 9 – 1 – 5? OR MAYBE 2 – 2 – 1?
9-4-7?
6-8-2?
1-9-5?
5-1-2?
4-0-4?
2-8-1?
0-0-7?
7-8-2?
HURRY NOW! OTHERWISE I HAVE TO GIVE YOU 0 OUT OF 10!
ERR... 392? NO! 597? MAYBE?
HERE, DEAREST TEACHER! WHAT LITTLE I HAVE, I GIVE TO YOU!
WHAT DID YOU EXPECT? GENEROSITY CAN'T BE TAUGHT!

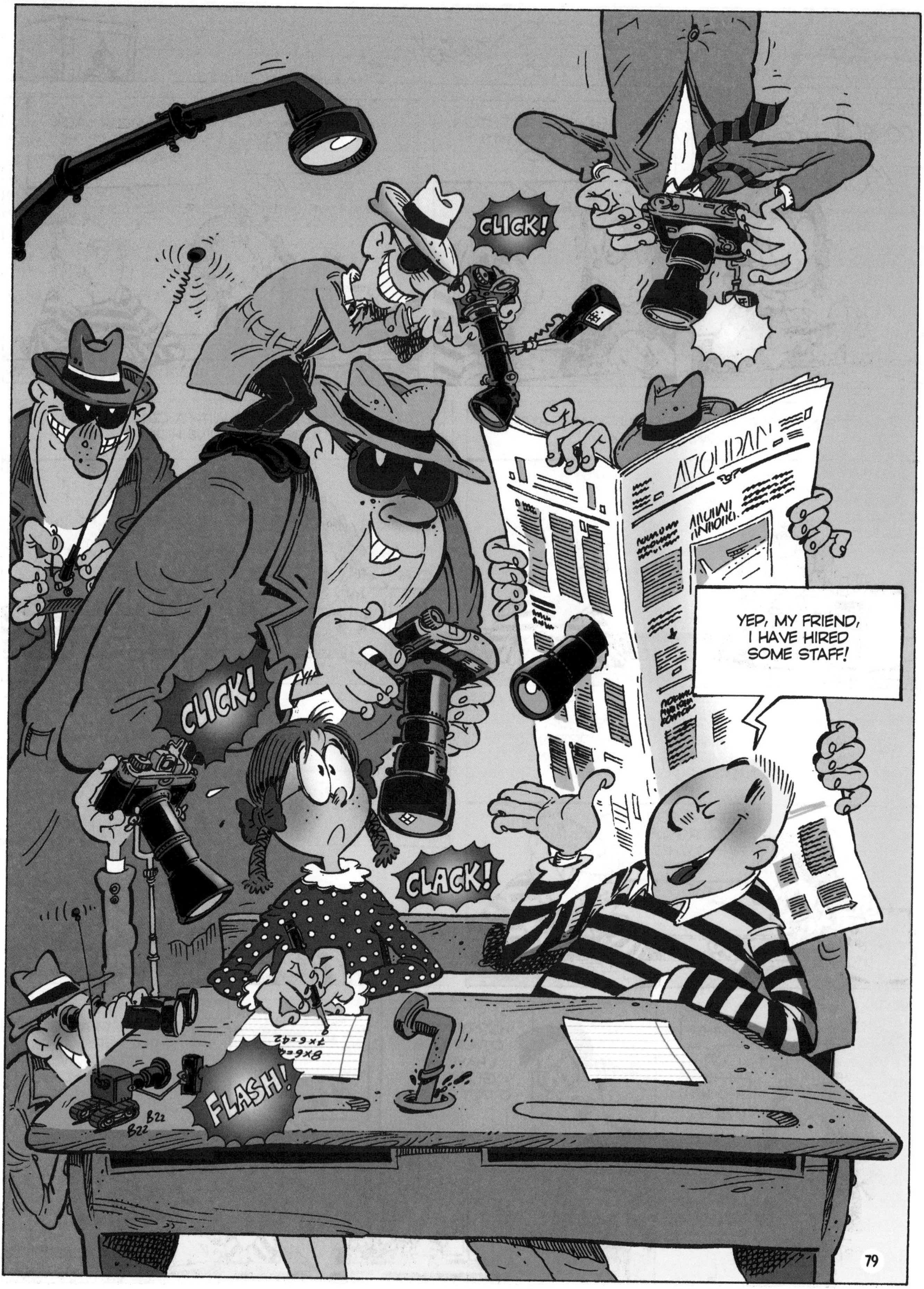
CLICK!
CLICK!
CLACK!
FLASH!
YEP, MY FRIEND, I HAVE HIRED SOME STAFF!
79

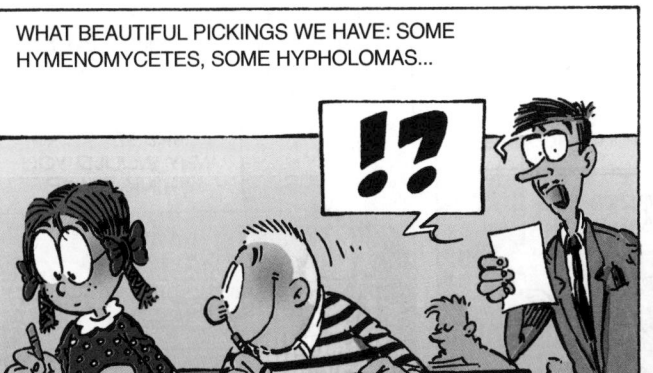

WHAT BEAUTIFUL PICKINGS WE HAVE: SOME HYMENOMYCETES, SOME HYPHOLOMAS...

!?

IN THE CORNER, DUCOBOO!

IN THE CORNER, PLEASE, DUCOBOO!

DID YOUR MOTHER NEVER TEACH YOU ANY MANNERS?

YOU'RE DOING A HUNDRED LINES FOR ME!

"WOULD YOU BE SO KIND AS TO DO ME 100 LINES?"

HE WANTS TO TEACH OTHER PEOPLE'S CHILDREN, YET ISN'T EVEN ABLE TO WATCH HIS OWN LANGUAGE?

STOP ANSWERING BACK! DUNCE!

SWEAR WORDS, NOW?!

OH, BRAVO! SETTING A FINE EXAMPLE!

GAH! BZZ! DZOING!

I'M SORRY, BUT MY KNOWLEDGE OF THE CHANG LANGUAGE ISN'T SUFFICIENT TO ALLOW ME TO UNDERSTAND THE ELEGANCE OF YOUR RESPONSE.

I BEG YOU, DUCOBOO! GO TO THE CORNER!

THAT'S BETTER! YOU JUST HAD TO ASK POLITELY!

YOU KNOW, SKELLY, SOMETIMES I WONDER IF HE'LL EVER LEARN!

IT CAN BE SO HARD TO TEACH THEM!

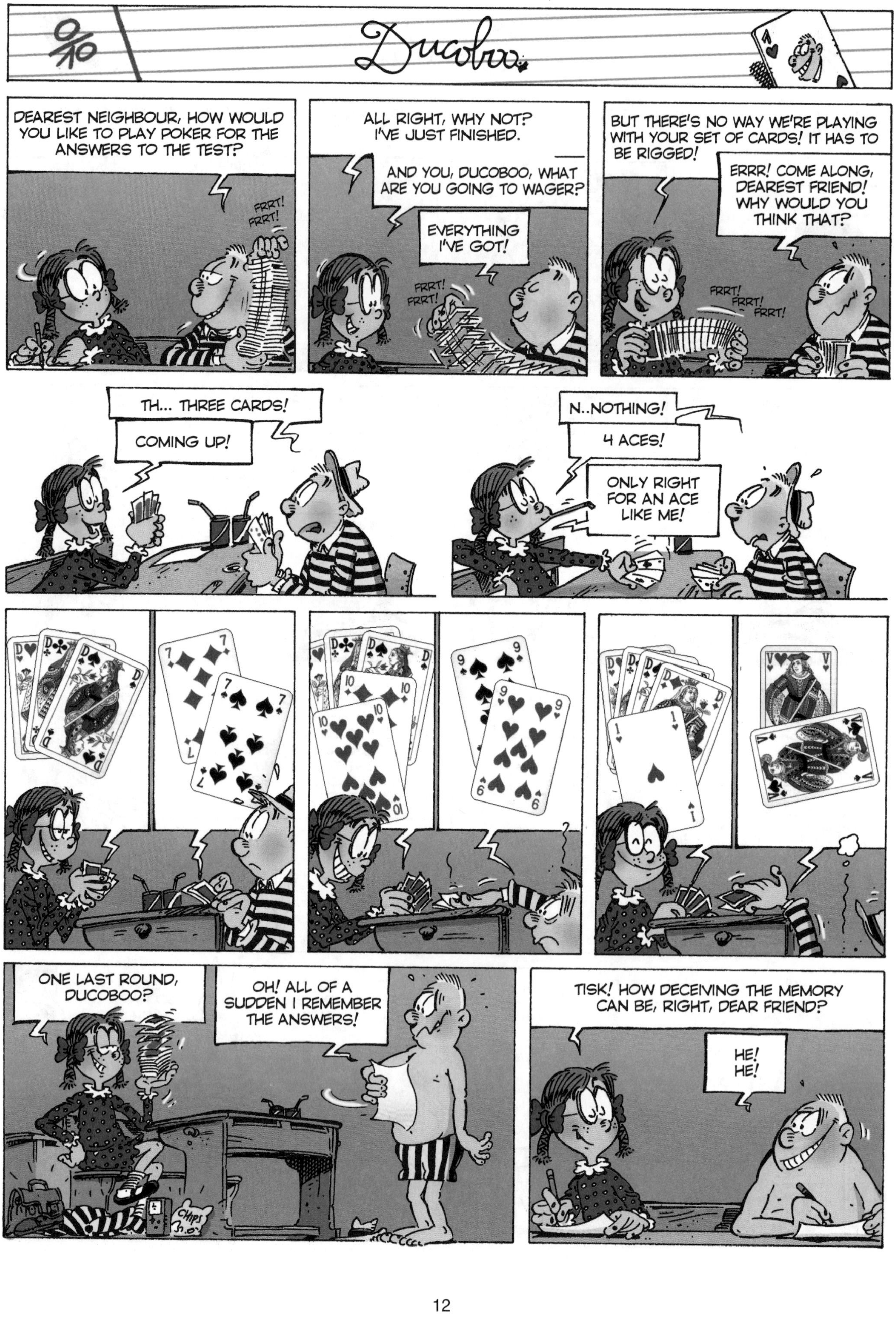
Ducoboo
DEAREST NEIGHBOUR, HOW WOULD YOU LIKE TO PLAY POKER FOR THE ANSWERS TO THE TEST?
FRRT! FRRT!
ALL RIGHT, WHY NOT? I'VE JUST FINISHED.
AND YOU, DUCOBOO, WHAT ARE YOU GOING TO WAGER?
EVERYTHING I'VE GOT!
FRRT! FRRT!
BUT THERE'S NO WAY WE'RE PLAYING WITH YOUR SET OF CARDS! IT HAS TO BE RIGGED!
ERRR! COME ALONG, DEAREST FRIEND! WHY WOULD YOU THINK THAT?
FRRT! FRRT! FRRT!
TH... THREE CARDS!
COMING UP!
N..NOTHING!
4 ACES!
ONLY RIGHT FOR AN ACE LIKE ME!
ONE LAST ROUND, DUCOBOO?
OH! ALL OF A SUDDEN I REMEMBER THE ANSWERS!
TISK! HOW DECEIVING THE MEMORY CAN BE, RIGHT, DEAR FRIEND?
HE! HE!

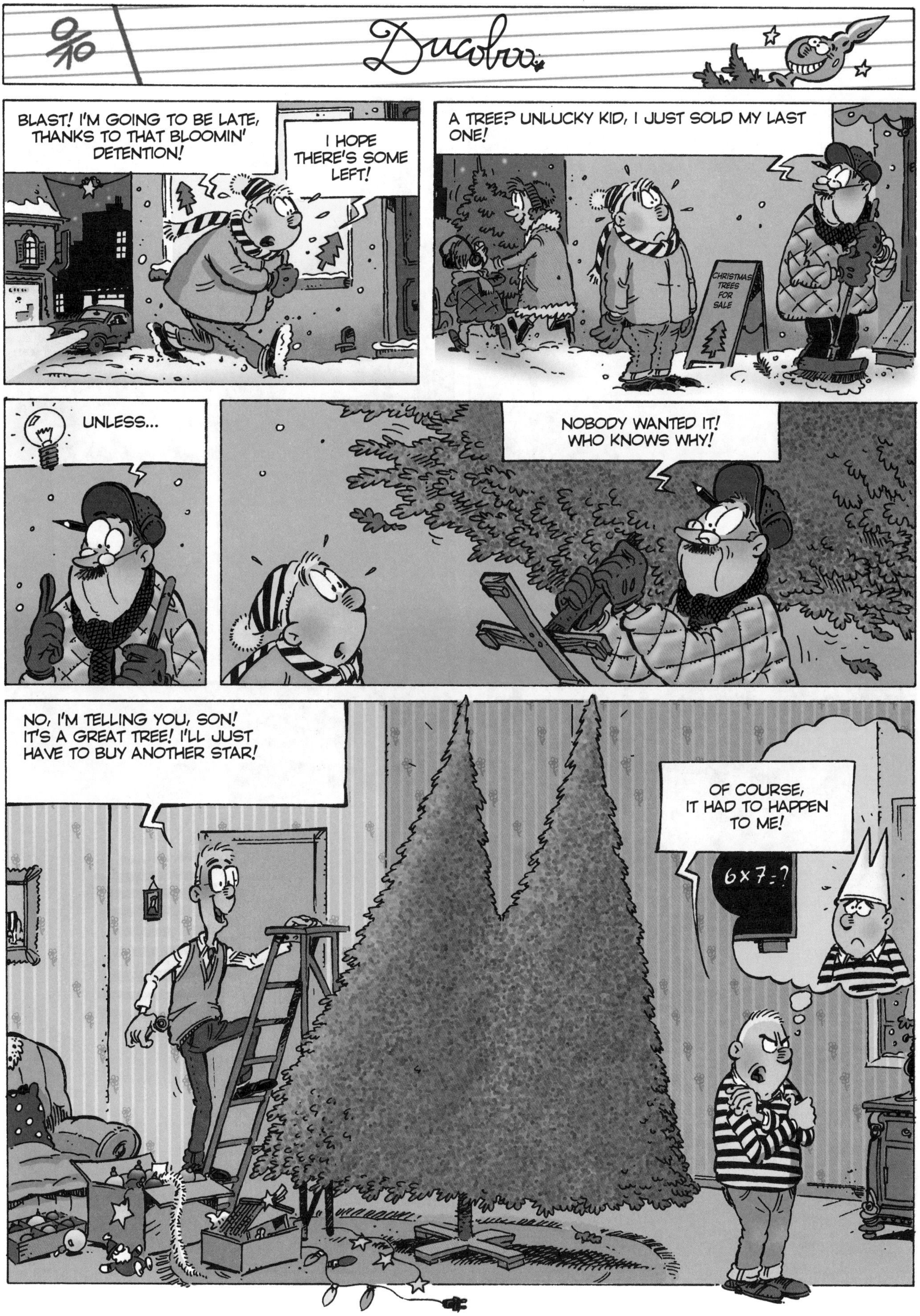

Ducobu
BLAST! I'M GOING TO BE LATE, THANKS TO THAT BLOOMIN' DETENTION!
I HOPE THERE'S SOME LEFT!
A TREE? UNLUCKY KID, I JUST SOLD MY LAST ONE!
CHRISTMAS TREES FOR SALE
UNLESS...
NOBODY WANTED IT! WHO KNOWS WHY!
NO, I'M TELLING YOU, SON! IT'S A GREAT TREE! I'LL JUST HAVE TO BUY ANOTHER STAR!
OF COURSE, IT HAD TO HAPPEN TO ME!
6×7=?

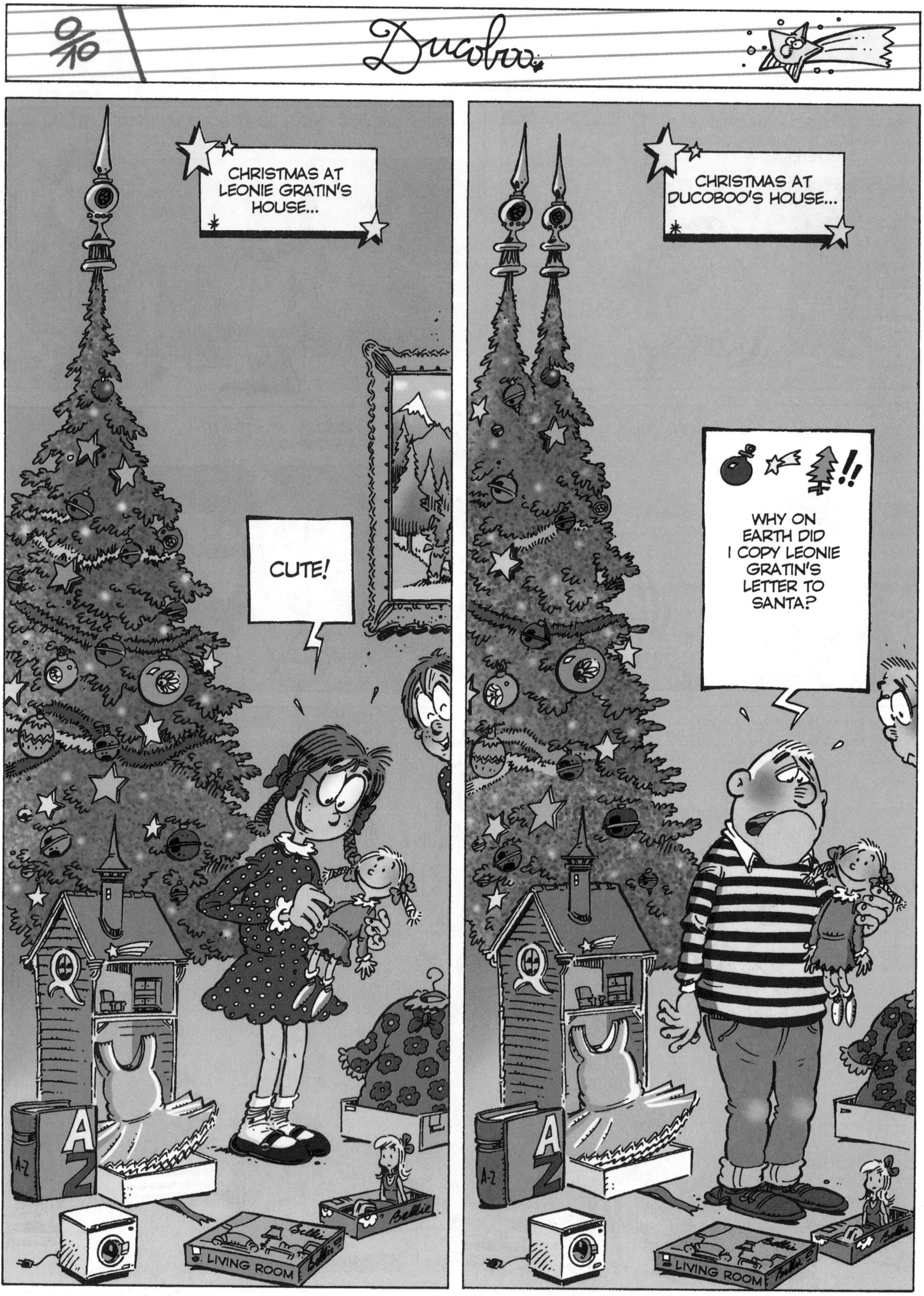
Ducoboo
CHRISTMAS AT LEONIE GRATIN'S HOUSE...
CUTE!
CHRISTMAS AT DUCOBOO'S HOUSE...
!!
WHY ON EARTH DID I COPY LEONIE GRATIN'S LETTER TO SANTA?
A-Z
LIVING ROOM
Bellie

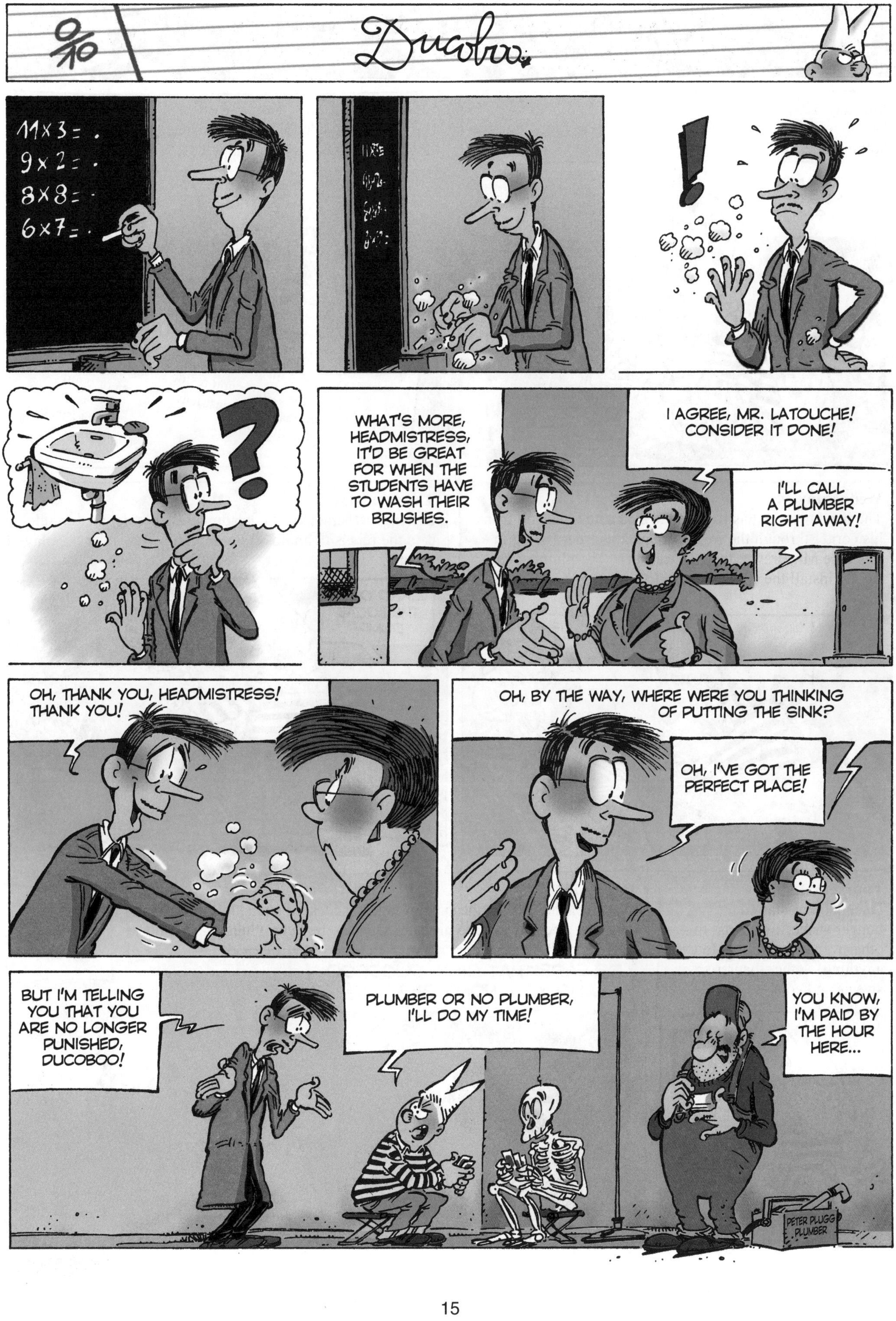
0/10
Ducoboo
11 x 3 = .
9 x 2 = .
8 x 8 = .
6 x 7 = .
WHAT'S MORE, HEADMISTRESS, IT'D BE GREAT FOR WHEN THE STUDENTS HAVE TO WASH THEIR BRUSHES.
I AGREE, MR. LATOUCHE! CONSIDER IT DONE!
I'LL CALL A PLUMBER RIGHT AWAY!
OH, THANK YOU, HEADMISTRESS! THANK YOU!
OH, BY THE WAY, WHERE WERE YOU THINKING OF PUTTING THE SINK?
OH, I'VE GOT THE PERFECT PLACE!
BUT I'M TELLING YOU THAT YOU ARE NO LONGER PUNISHED, DUCOBOO!
PLUMBER OR NO PLUMBER, I'LL DO MY TIME!
YOU KNOW, I'M PAID BY THE HOUR HERE...
PETER PLUGG PLUMBER

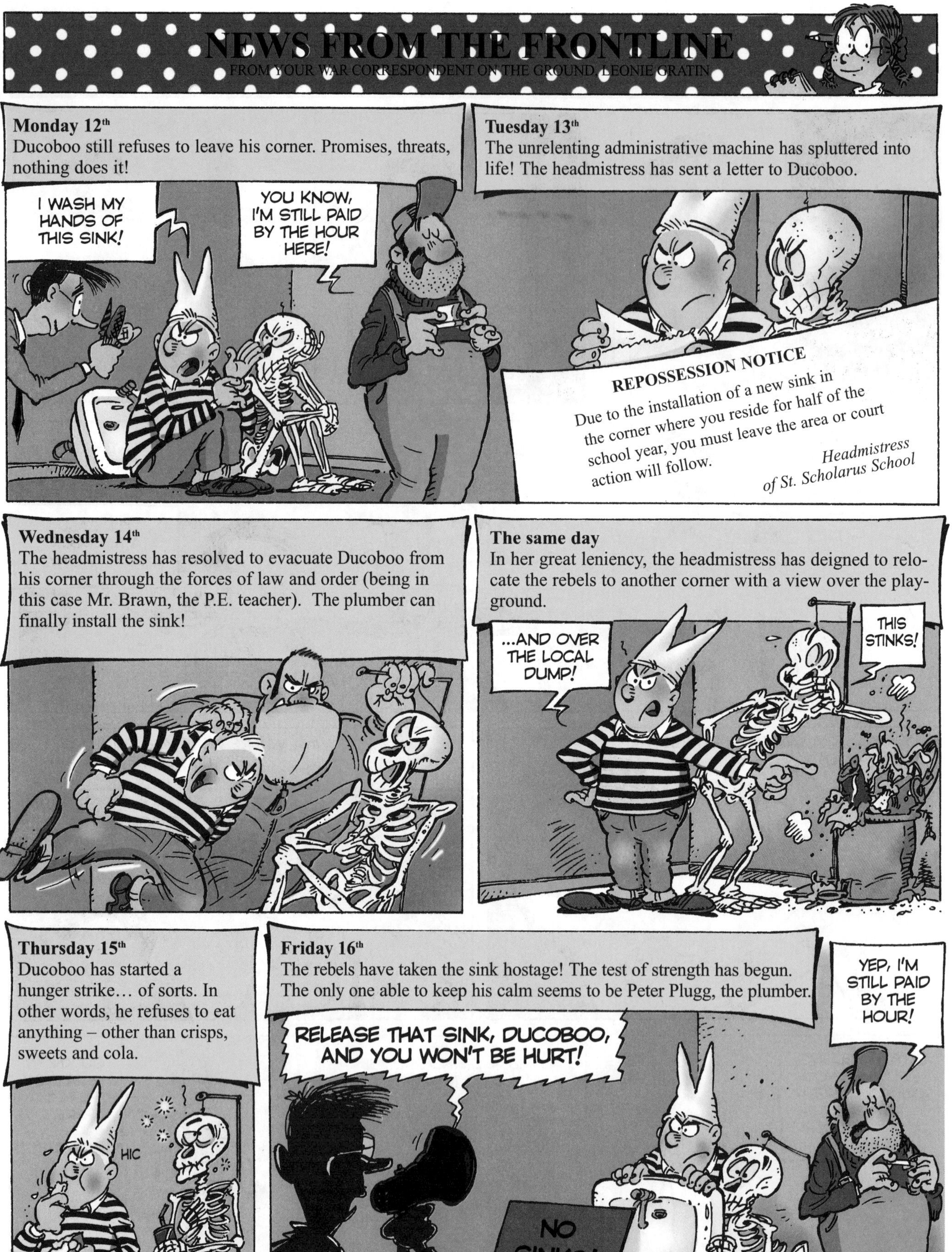
NEWS FROM THE FRONTLINE
FROM YOUR WAR CORRESPONDENT ON THE GROUND, LEONIE GRATIN
Monday 12th
Ducoboo still refuses to leave his corner. Promises, threats, nothing does it!
I WASH MY HANDS OF THIS SINK!
YOU KNOW, I'M STILL PAID BY THE HOUR HERE!
Tuesday 13th
The unrelenting administrative machine has spluttered into life! The headmistress has sent a letter to Ducoboo.
REPOSSESSION NOTICE
Due to the installation of a new sink in the corner where you reside for half of the school year, you must leave the area or court action will follow.
Headmistress of St. Scholarus School
Wednesday 14th
The headmistress has resolved to evacuate Ducoboo from his corner through the forces of law and order (being in this case Mr. Brawn, the P.E. teacher). The plumber can finally install the sink!
The same day
In her great leniency, the headmistress has deigned to relocate the rebels to another corner with a view over the playground.
...AND OVER THE LOCAL DUMP!
THIS STINKS!
Thursday 15th
Ducoboo has started a hunger strike… of sorts. In other words, he refuses to eat anything – other than crisps, sweets and cola.
HIC
Friday 16th
The rebels have taken the sink hostage! The test of strength has begun. The only one able to keep his calm seems to be Peter Plugg, the plumber.
RELEASE THAT SINK, DUCOBOO, AND YOU WON'T BE HURT!
YEP, I'M STILL PAID BY THE HOUR!
NO SINKS!

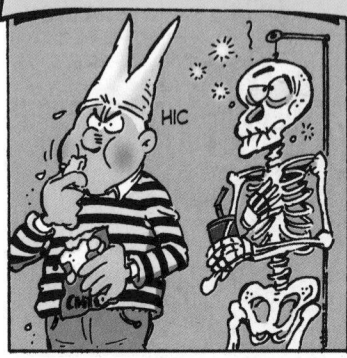

NEWS FROM THE FRONTLINE

FROM YOUR WAR CORRESPONDENT ON THE GROUND: LEONIE GRATIN (CONTINUED)

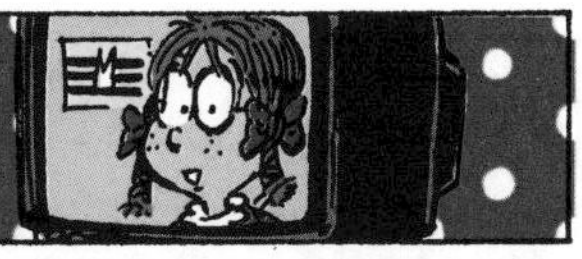

Monday 19th
Incredible! At dawn this morning, the rebels proclaimed their corner's independence! Will the War of the Sink take an international turn?

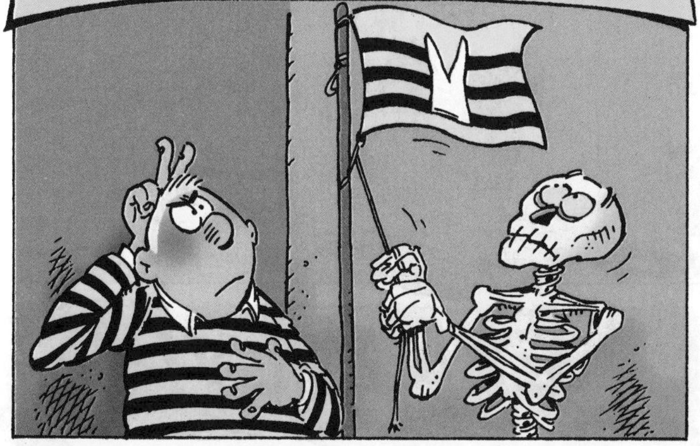

Tuesday 20th
By unanimous vote, the United Nations has recognized Ducoland as a sovereign state. It is the smallest state in the world as of today!

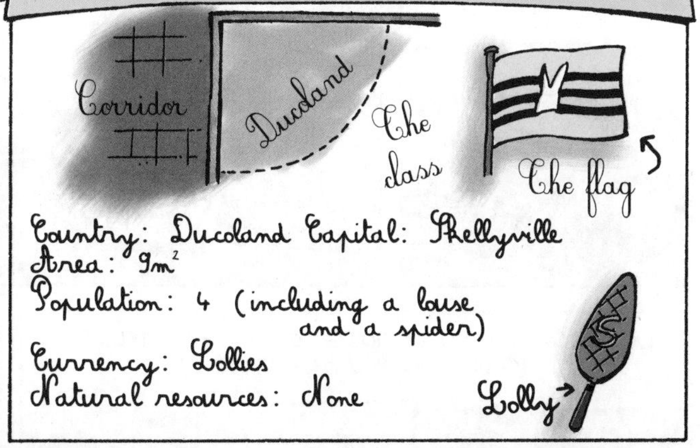
Corridor
Ducoland
The class
The flag
Country: Ducoland Capital: Skellyville
Area: 9m²
Population: 4 (including a louse and a spider)
Currency: Lollies
Natural resources: None
Lolly

Wednesday 21st
This morning, in the presence of several foreign heads of state, the Ducoland president made his inaugural speech.

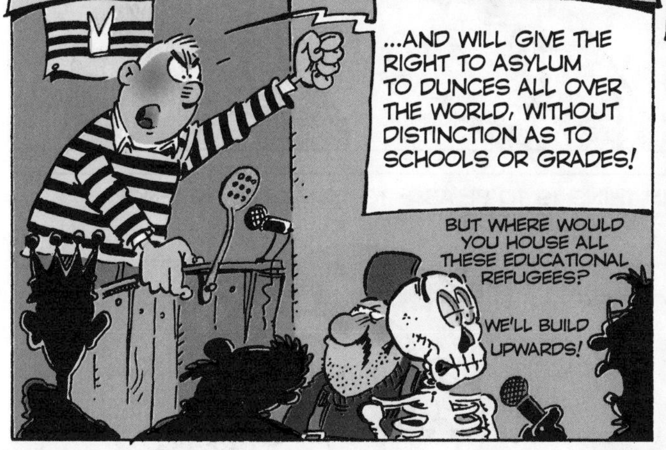
...AND WILL GIVE THE RIGHT TO ASYLUM TO DUNCES ALL OVER THE WORLD, WITHOUT DISTINCTION AS TO SCHOOLS OR GRADES!
BUT WHERE WOULD YOU HOUSE ALL THESE EDUCATIONAL REFUGEES?
WE'LL BUILD UPWARDS!

Thursday 22nd
A mediator has been sent by the United Nations to try and end the conflict that has lasted two weeks between St. Scholarus School and Ducoland.

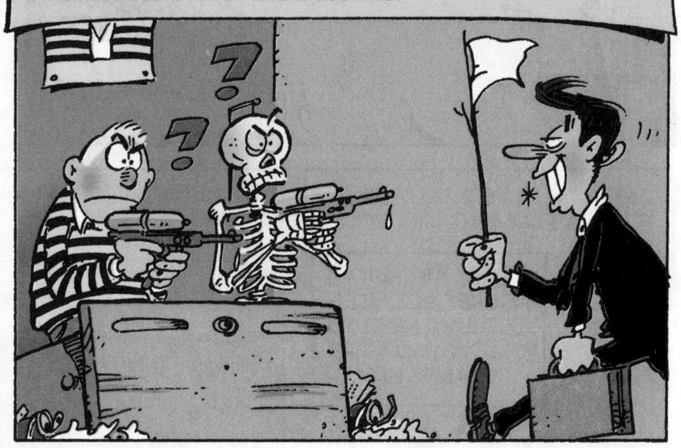

Friday 23rd
After intense negotiations, the peace accords have finally been signed! St. Scholarus School will be able to install the sink on Ducoland territory!

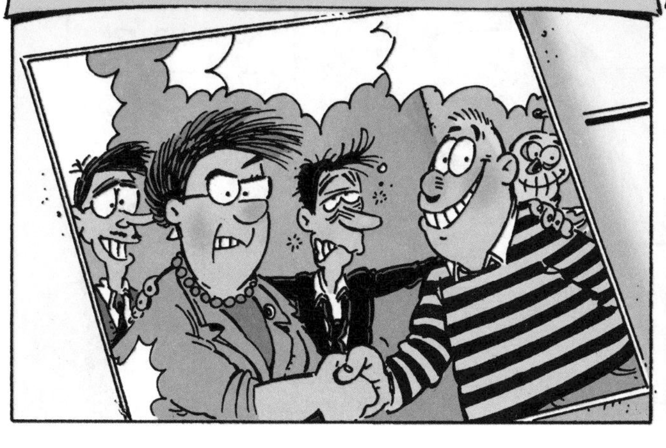

That day
As compensation, the embargo on lollies will be lifted and the Ducoland population will be exempt from any homework until the end of the school year!

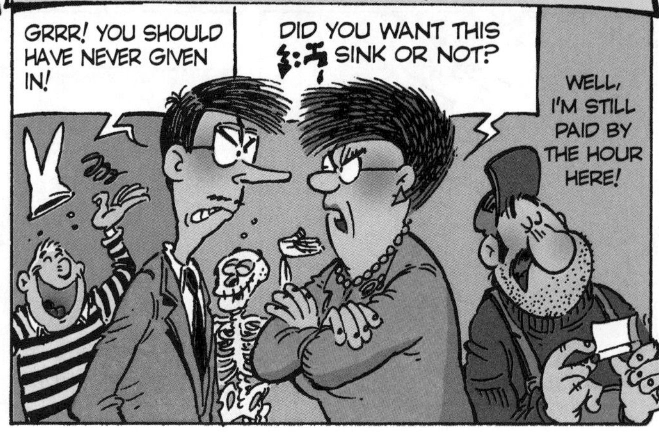
GRRR! YOU SHOULD HAVE NEVER GIVEN IN!
DID YOU WANT THIS SINK OR NOT?
WELL, I'M STILL PAID BY THE HOUR HERE!

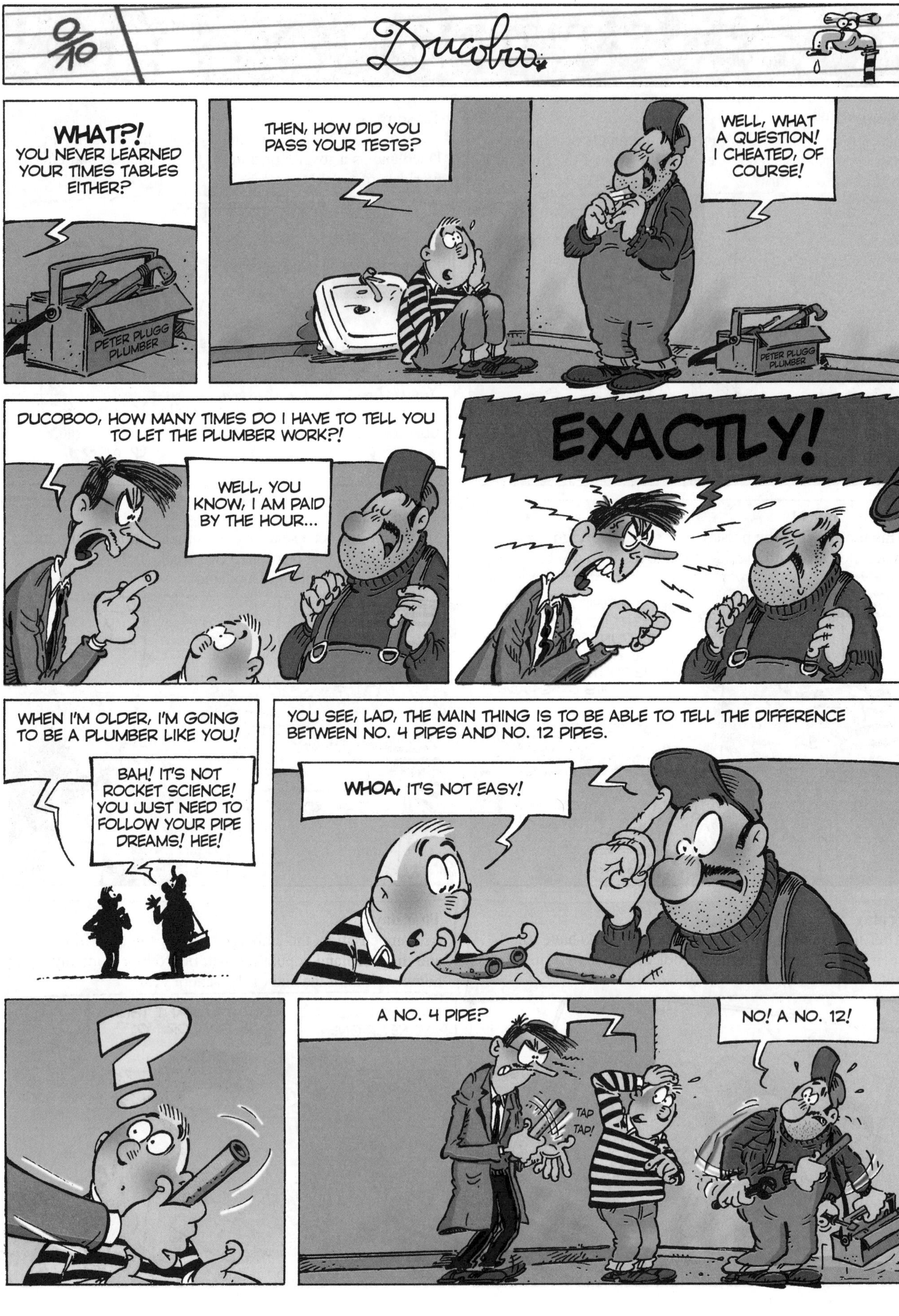

2/10
Ducoboo
WHAT?! YOU NEVER LEARNED YOUR TIMES TABLES EITHER?
PETER PLUGG PLUMBER
THEN, HOW DID YOU PASS YOUR TESTS?
WELL, WHAT A QUESTION! I CHEATED, OF COURSE!
PETER PLUGG PLUMBER
DUCOBOO, HOW MANY TIMES DO I HAVE TO TELL YOU TO LET THE PLUMBER WORK?!
WELL, YOU KNOW, I AM PAID BY THE HOUR...
EXACTLY!
WHEN I'M OLDER, I'M GOING TO BE A PLUMBER LIKE YOU!
BAH! IT'S NOT ROCKET SCIENCE! YOU JUST NEED TO FOLLOW YOUR PIPE DREAMS! HEE!
YOU SEE, LAD, THE MAIN THING IS TO BE ABLE TO TELL THE DIFFERENCE BETWEEN NO. 4 PIPES AND NO. 12 PIPES.
WHOA, IT'S NOT EASY!
A NO. 4 PIPE?
NO! A NO. 12!
TAP TAP!

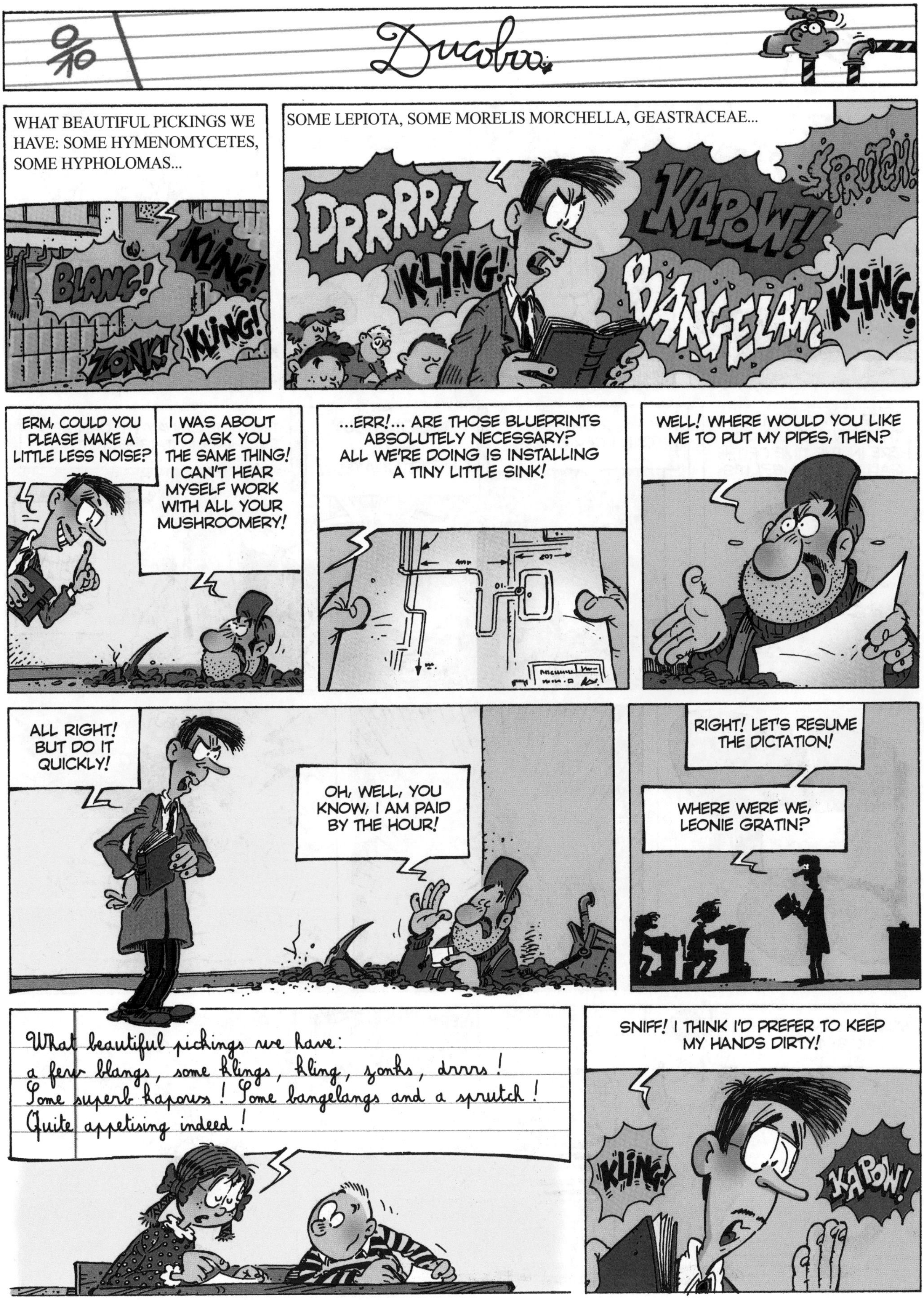
0/10
Ducobu
WHAT BEAUTIFUL PICKINGS WE HAVE: SOME HYMENOMYCETES, SOME HYPHOLOMAS...
BLANG!
KLING!
ZONK!
KLING!
SOME LEPIOTA, SOME MORELIS MORCHELLA, GEASTRACEAE...
DRRRR!
KLING!
KAPOW!
SPRUTCH!
BANGELANG!
KLING!
ERM, COULD YOU PLEASE MAKE A LITTLE LESS NOISE?
I WAS ABOUT TO ASK YOU THE SAME THING! I CAN'T HEAR MYSELF WORK WITH ALL YOUR MUSHROOMERY!
...ERR!... ARE THOSE BLUEPRINTS ABSOLUTELY NECESSARY? ALL WE'RE DOING IS INSTALLING A TINY LITTLE SINK!
WELL! WHERE WOULD YOU LIKE ME TO PUT MY PIPES, THEN?
ALL RIGHT! BUT DO IT QUICKLY!
OH, WELL, YOU KNOW, I AM PAID BY THE HOUR!
RIGHT! LET'S RESUME THE DICTATION!
WHERE WERE WE, LEONIE GRATIN?
What beautiful pickings we have:
a few blangs, some klings, kling, zonks, drrrs!
Some superb kapows! Some bangelangs and a sprutch!
Quite appetising indeed!
SNIFF! I THINK I'D PREFER TO KEEP MY HANDS DIRTY!
KLING!
KAPOW!

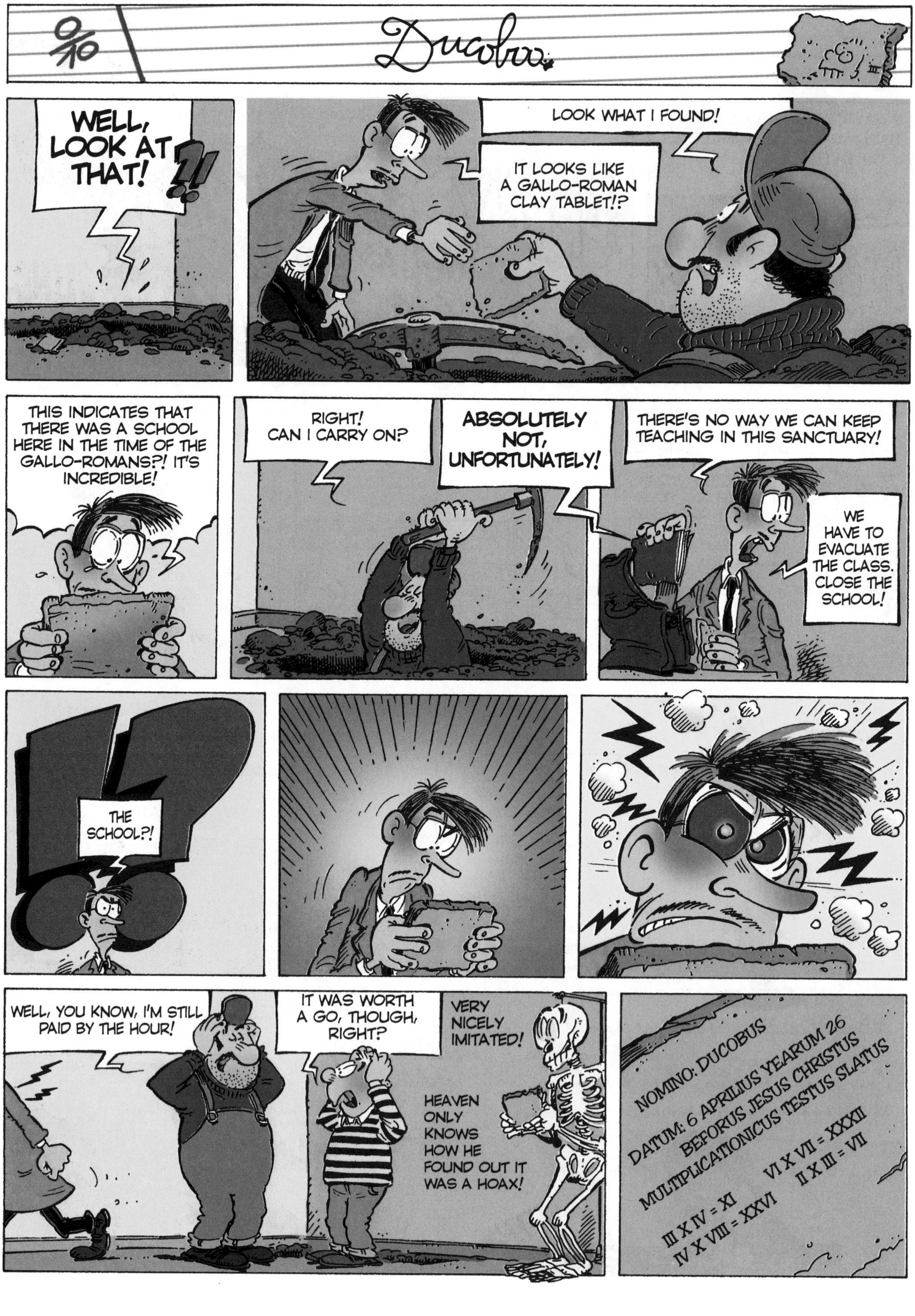
Ducobu
WELL, LOOK AT THAT! ?!
LOOK WHAT I FOUND!
IT LOOKS LIKE A GALLO-ROMAN CLAY TABLET!?
THIS INDICATES THAT THERE WAS A SCHOOL HERE IN THE TIME OF THE GALLO-ROMANS?! IT'S INCREDIBLE!
RIGHT! CAN I CARRY ON?
ABSOLUTELY NOT, UNFORTUNATELY!
THERE'S NO WAY WE CAN KEEP TEACHING IN THIS SANCTUARY!
WE HAVE TO EVACUATE THE CLASS. CLOSE THE SCHOOL!
THE SCHOOL?!
WELL, YOU KNOW, I'M STILL PAID BY THE HOUR!
IT WAS WORTH A GO, THOUGH, RIGHT?
VERY NICELY IMITATED!
HEAVEN ONLY KNOWS HOW HE FOUND OUT IT WAS A HOAX!
NOMINO: DUCOBUS
DATUM: 6 APRILIUS YEARUM 26 BEFORUS JESUS CHRISTUS
MULTIPLICATIONICUS TESTUS SLATUS
III X IV = XI
IV X VIII = XXVI
VI X VII = XXXII
II X III = VII

Problem:
Achilles runs a bath.
But the bath has a leak.
Knowing that the hot water tap
delivers 3 litres a minute, and that
the bathtub has a capacity of 0.8m³
but loses 20cl every half an hour
how long does Achilles need to
fill his bathtub?

THE FIRST ONE TO FIND THE ANSWER, RAISE YOUR HAND.

ERR... YES?

RIGHT! WELL! FIRST THING TO DO, OF COURSE, IS TO TURN OFF THE TAP!

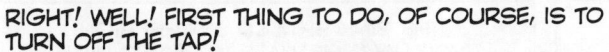

THEN, YOU SEAL THE CRACK WITH A GOOD LAYER OF WATERPROOF SEALANT AND BOB'S YOUR UNCLE!

MORE!

CLAP! CLAP! CLAP!

BRAVO!

A... AN INVOICE!?!

WHAT?!! I REPAIRED YOUR LEAKY OLD BATHTUB, DIDN'T I?!

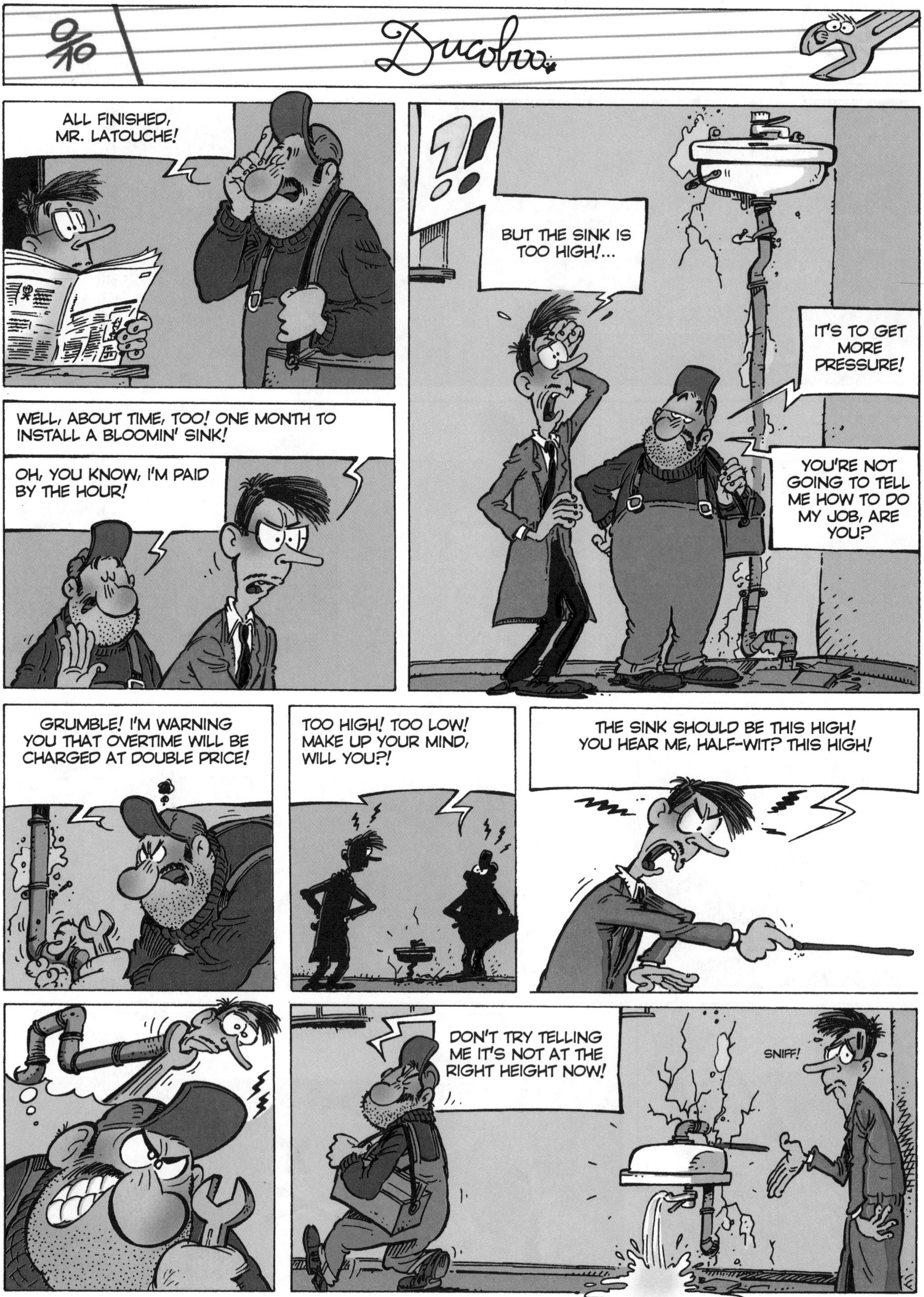
Ducobu
ALL FINISHED, MR. LATOUCHE!
?!
BUT THE SINK IS TOO HIGH!...
IT'S TO GET MORE PRESSURE!
YOU'RE NOT GOING TO TELL ME HOW TO DO MY JOB, ARE YOU?
WELL, ABOUT TIME, TOO! ONE MONTH TO INSTALL A BLOOMIN' SINK!
OH, YOU KNOW, I'M PAID BY THE HOUR!
GRUMBLE! I'M WARNING YOU THAT OVERTIME WILL BE CHARGED AT DOUBLE PRICE!
TOO HIGH! TOO LOW! MAKE UP YOUR MIND, WILL YOU?!
THE SINK SHOULD BE THIS HIGH! YOU HEAR ME, HALF-WIT? THIS HIGH!
DON'T TRY TELLING ME IT'S NOT AT THE RIGHT HEIGHT NOW!
SNIFF!

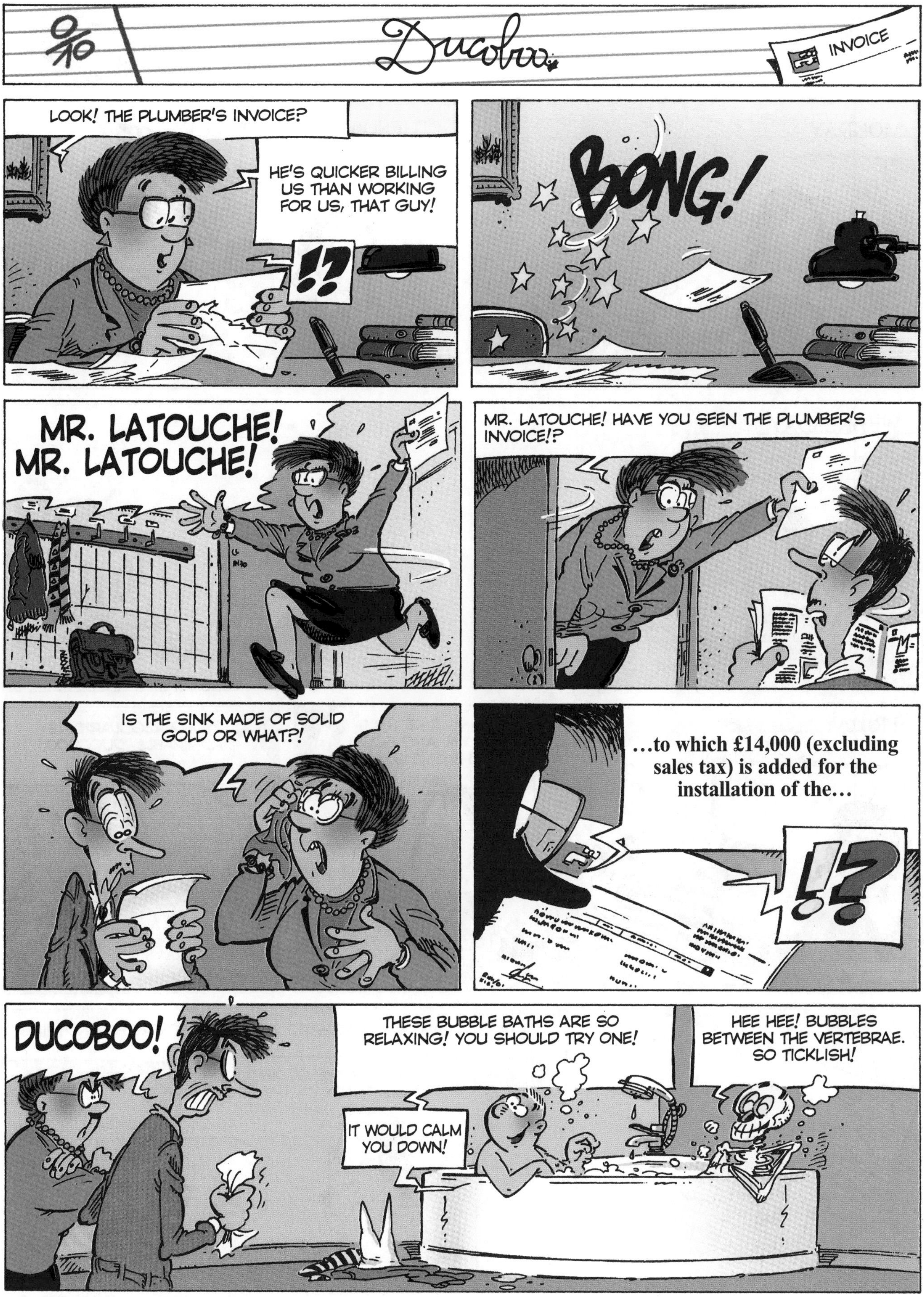

0/10
Ducoboo
INVOICE
LOOK! THE PLUMBER'S INVOICE?
HE'S QUICKER BILLING US THAN WORKING FOR US, THAT GUY!
!?
BONG!
MR. LATOUCHE! MR. LATOUCHE!
MR. LATOUCHE! HAVE YOU SEEN THE PLUMBER'S INVOICE!?
IS THE SINK MADE OF SOLID GOLD OR WHAT?!
…to which £14,000 (excluding sales tax) is added for the installation of the…
!?
DUCOBOO!
THESE BUBBLE BATHS ARE SO RELAXING! YOU SHOULD TRY ONE!
IT WOULD CALM YOU DOWN!
HEE HEE! BUBBLES BETWEEN THE VERTEBRAE. SO TICKLISH!

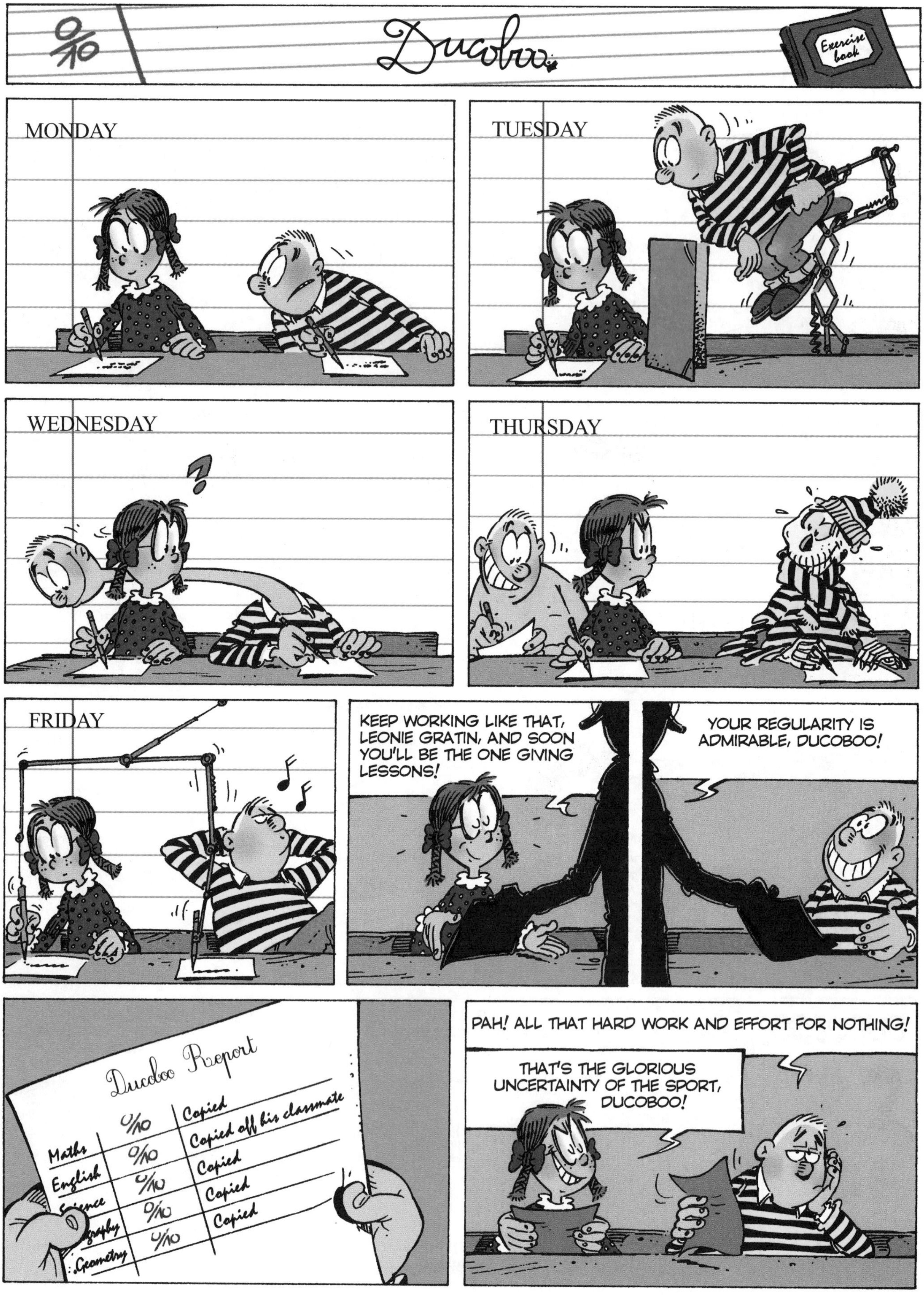
0/10
Ducoboo
Exercise book
MONDAY
TUESDAY
WEDNESDAY
THURSDAY
FRIDAY
KEEP WORKING LIKE THAT, LEONIE GRATIN, AND SOON YOU'LL BE THE ONE GIVING LESSONS!
YOUR REGULARITY IS ADMIRABLE, DUCOBOO!
Ducoboo Report
0/10 Copied
Maths 0/10 Copied off his classmate
English 0/10 Copied
Science 0/10 Copied
Geometry 0/10 Copied
PAH! ALL THAT HARD WORK AND EFFORT FOR NOTHING!
THAT'S THE GLORIOUS UNCERTAINTY OF THE SPORT, DUCOBOO!

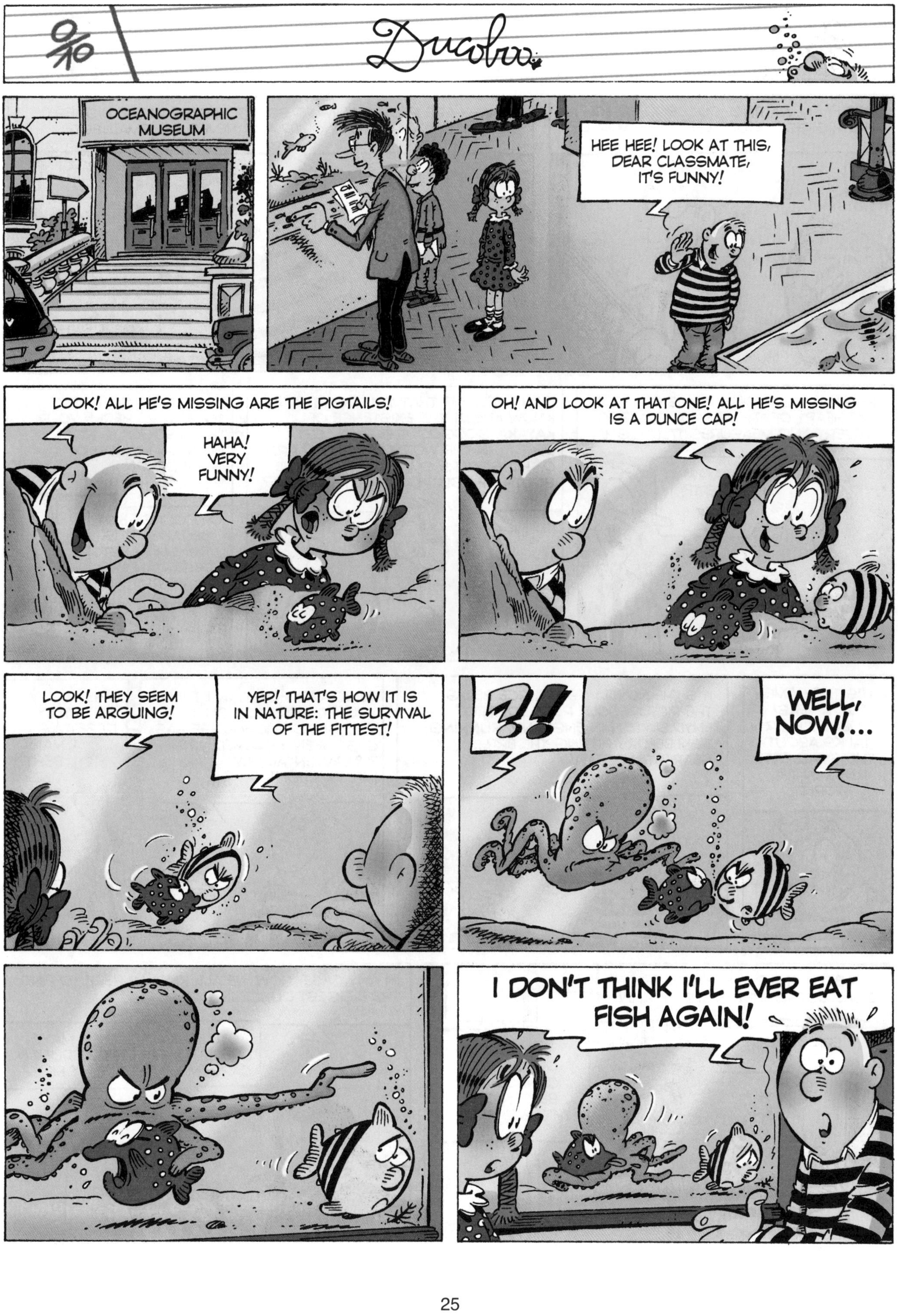

Ducobu
OCEANOGRAPHIC MUSEUM
HEE HEE! LOOK AT THIS, DEAR CLASSMATE, IT'S FUNNY!
LOOK! ALL HE'S MISSING ARE THE PIGTAILS!
HAHA! VERY FUNNY!
OH! AND LOOK AT THAT ONE! ALL HE'S MISSING IS A DUNCE CAP!
LOOK! THEY SEEM TO BE ARGUING!
YEP! THAT'S HOW IT IS IN NATURE: THE SURVIVAL OF THE FITTEST!
?!
WELL, NOW!...
I DON'T THINK I'LL EVER EAT FISH AGAIN!

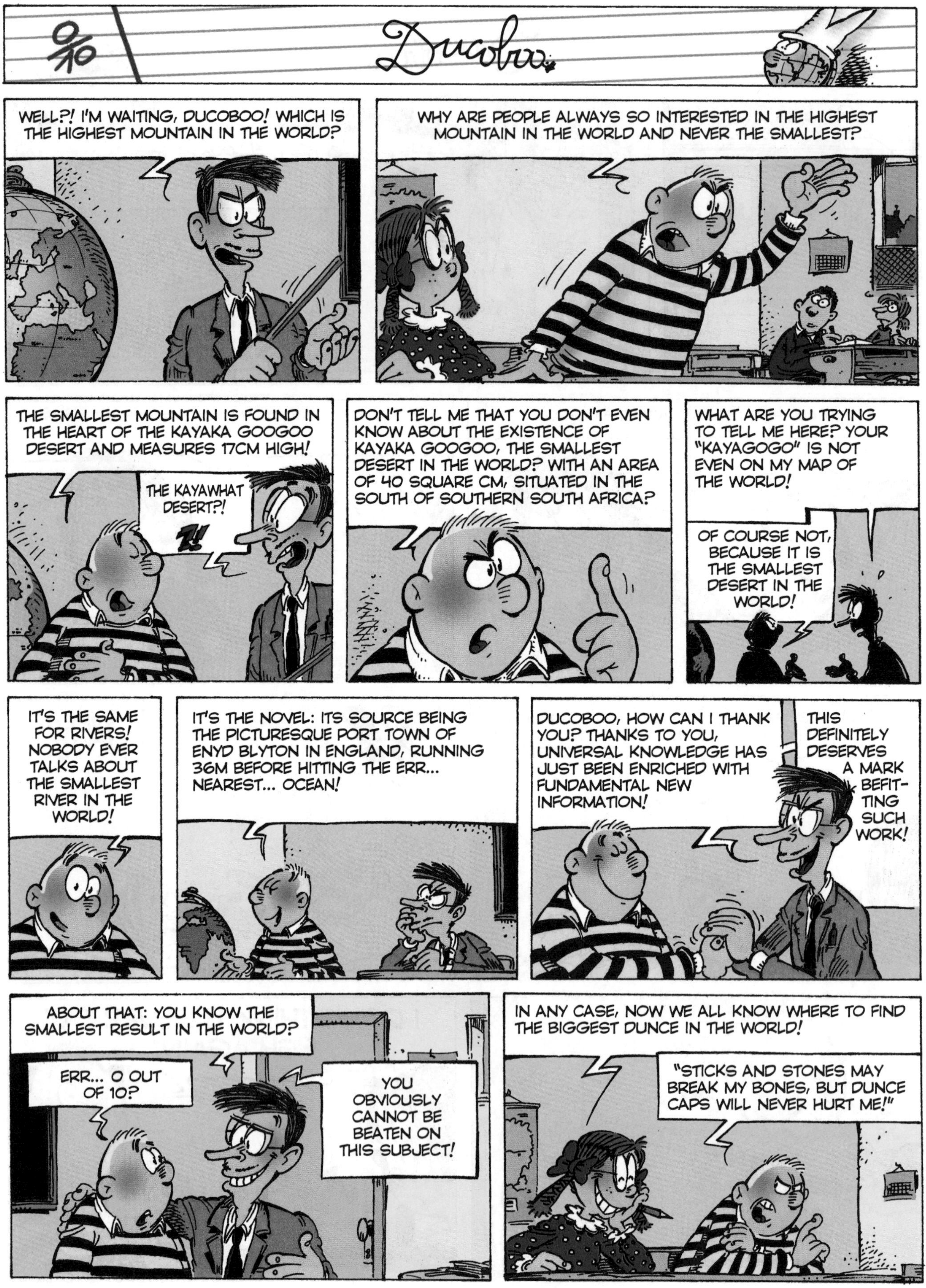
0/10
Ducobu
WELL?! I'M WAITING, DUCOBOO! WHICH IS THE HIGHEST MOUNTAIN IN THE WORLD?
WHY ARE PEOPLE ALWAYS SO INTERESTED IN THE HIGHEST MOUNTAIN IN THE WORLD AND NEVER THE SMALLEST?
THE SMALLEST MOUNTAIN IS FOUND IN THE HEART OF THE KAYAKA GOOGOO DESERT AND MEASURES 17CM HIGH!
THE KAYAWHAT DESERT?!
DON'T TELL ME THAT YOU DON'T EVEN KNOW ABOUT THE EXISTENCE OF KAYAKA GOOGOO, THE SMALLEST DESERT IN THE WORLD? WITH AN AREA OF 40 SQUARE CM, SITUATED IN THE SOUTH OF SOUTHERN SOUTH AFRICA?
WHAT ARE YOU TRYING TO TELL ME HERE? YOUR "KAYAGOGO" IS NOT EVEN ON MY MAP OF THE WORLD!
OF COURSE NOT, BECAUSE IT IS THE SMALLEST DESERT IN THE WORLD!
IT'S THE SAME FOR RIVERS! NOBODY EVER TALKS ABOUT THE SMALLEST RIVER IN THE WORLD!
IT'S THE NOVEL: ITS SOURCE BEING THE PICTURESQUE PORT TOWN OF ENYD BLYTON IN ENGLAND, RUNNING 36M BEFORE HITTING THE ERR... NEAREST... OCEAN!
DUCOBOO, HOW CAN I THANK YOU? THANKS TO YOU, UNIVERSAL KNOWLEDGE HAS JUST BEEN ENRICHED WITH FUNDAMENTAL NEW INFORMATION!
THIS DEFINITELY DESERVES A MARK BEFIT-TING SUCH WORK!
ABOUT THAT: YOU KNOW THE SMALLEST RESULT IN THE WORLD?
ERR... 0 OUT OF 10?
YOU OBVIOUSLY CANNOT BE BEATEN ON THIS SUBJECT!
IN ANY CASE, NOW WE ALL KNOW WHERE TO FIND THE BIGGEST DUNCE IN THE WORLD!
"STICKS AND STONES MAY BREAK MY BONES, BUT DUNCE CAPS WILL NEVER HURT ME!"

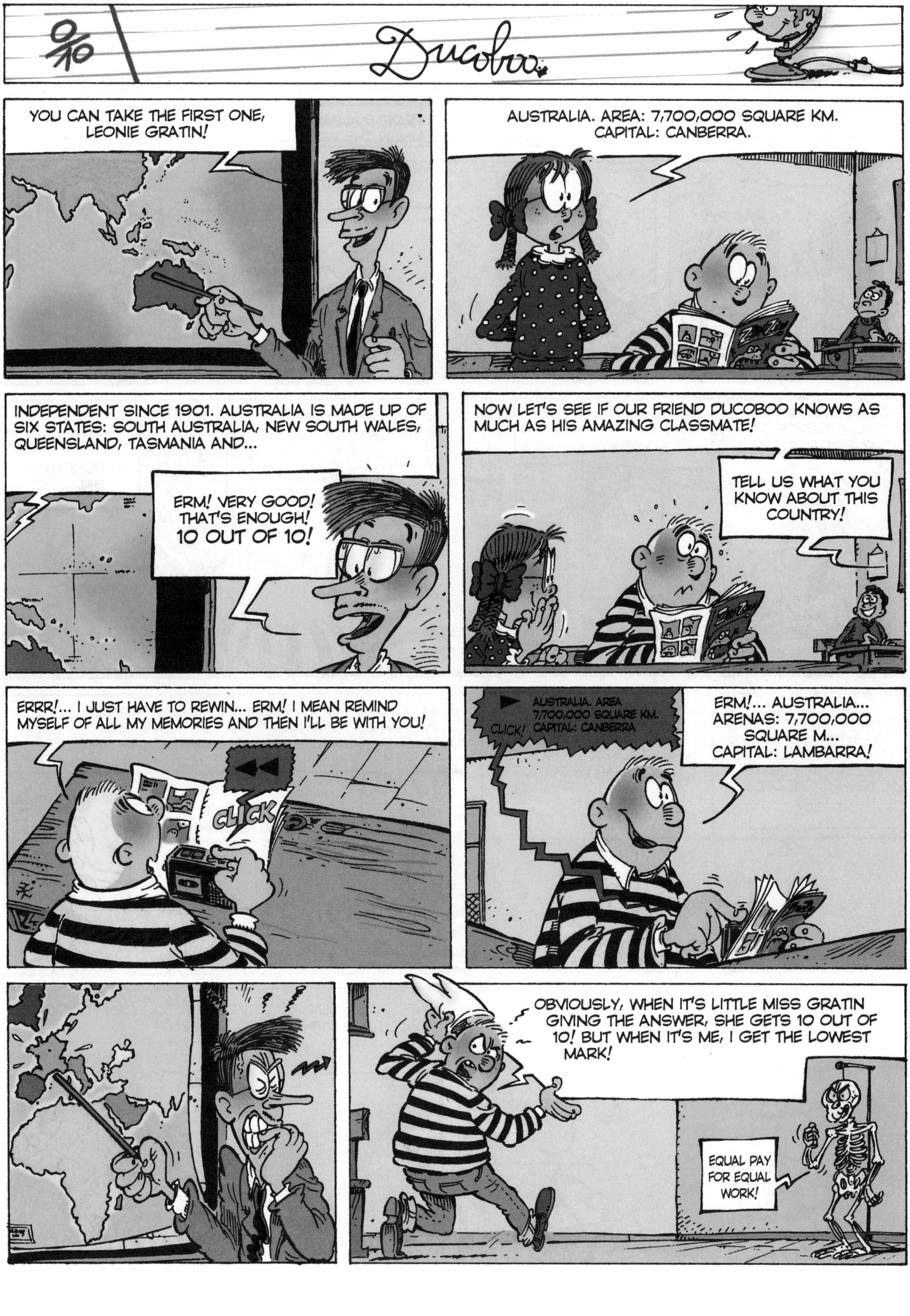
9/10
Ducoboo
YOU CAN TAKE THE FIRST ONE, LEONIE GRATIN!
AUSTRALIA. AREA: 7,700,000 SQUARE KM. CAPITAL: CANBERRA.
INDEPENDENT SINCE 1901. AUSTRALIA IS MADE UP OF SIX STATES: SOUTH AUSTRALIA, NEW SOUTH WALES, QUEENSLAND, TASMANIA AND...
ERM! VERY GOOD! THAT'S ENOUGH! 10 OUT OF 10!
NOW LET'S SEE IF OUR FRIEND DUCOBOO KNOWS AS MUCH AS HIS AMAZING CLASSMATE!
TELL US WHAT YOU KNOW ABOUT THIS COUNTRY!
ERRR!... I JUST HAVE TO REWIN... ERM! I MEAN REMIND MYSELF OF ALL MY MEMORIES AND THEN I'LL BE WITH YOU!
CLICK
CLICK! AUSTRALIA. AREA 7,700,000 SQUARE KM. CAPITAL: CANBERRA
ERM!... AUSTRALIA... ARENAS: 7,700,000 SQUARE M... CAPITAL: LAMBARRA!
OBVIOUSLY, WHEN IT'S LITTLE MISS GRATIN GIVING THE ANSWER, SHE GETS 10 OUT OF 10! BUT WHEN IT'S ME, I GET THE LOWEST MARK!
EQUAL PAY FOR EQUAL WORK!

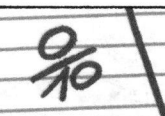

WHAT BEAUTIFUL PICKINGS WE HAVE: SOME HYMENOMYCETES, SOME HYPHOLOMAS...

HAPPY BIRTHDAY MR. LATOUCHE!

THAT... THAT... THAT'S FOR ME?

I CAN'T GUARANTEE THAT THERE'S THE RIGHT NUMBER OF CANDLES ON IT!

PERHAPS YOU'D ALREADY NOTICED: MATHS AND I DON'T GET ALONG!

WAIT! THAT'S NOT ALL! THERE'S A PRESENT, TOO!

A PREPRE... A PRESENT?

FOR THE DAYS WHEN I DRIVE YOU CRAZY...

A PUNCHING BALL?!?

HOW NICE OF YOU TO THINK OF ME ON MY BIRTHDAY! SOB! TO TELL THE TRUTH, YOU'RE THE ONLY ONE.

I SUPPOSE IT'S TRUE THAT CERTAIN PEOPLE ARE QUICKER TO EXTORT GOOD MARKS OUT OF YOU THAN TO GIVE YOU PRESENTS...

ERM!... ABOUT THAT, BIRTHDAY BOY... FOR THAT PUNISHMENT HOMEWORK THAT WAS DUE TODAY, I HAVE HAD, SO TO SPEAK, A SLIGHT DELAY AND...

I'LL HEAR NO MORE OF IT! IT'S MY BIRTHDAY—I'LL LET YOU OFF THE HOOK!

WAIT A MINUTE! MY BIRTHDAY WAS FOUR MONTHS AGO!

REALLY? HE! HE! I'M NOT SO GOOD WITH DATES!

WELL, ON YOUR REAL BIRTHDAY, YOU CAN FORGET ABOUT ME GIVING YOU A PRESENT!

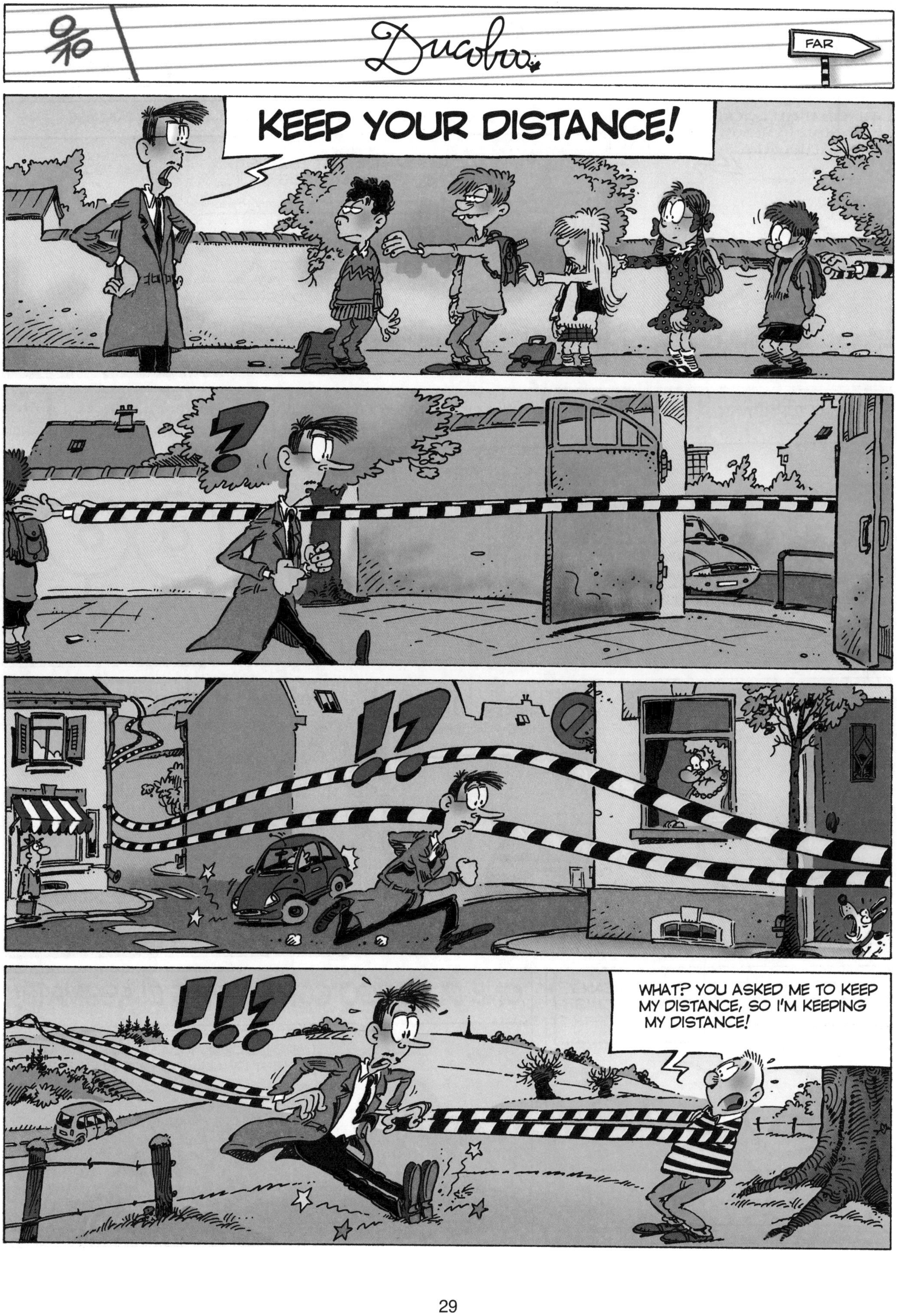
0/10
Ducobu
FAR
KEEP YOUR DISTANCE!
WHAT? YOU ASKED ME TO KEEP MY DISTANCE, SO I'M KEEPING MY DISTANCE!

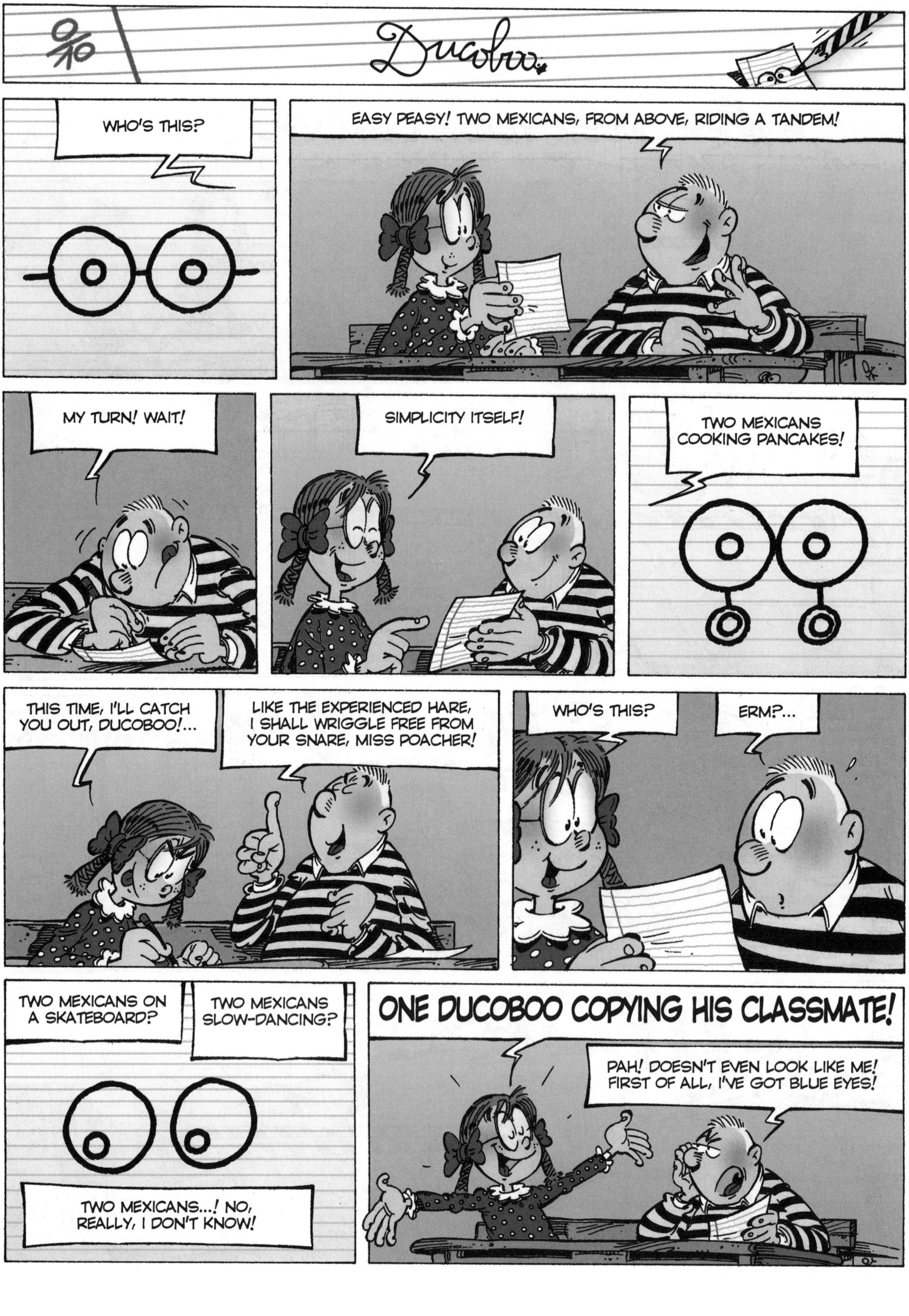
Ducoboo
WHO'S THIS?
EASY PEASY! TWO MEXICANS, FROM ABOVE, RIDING A TANDEM!
MY TURN! WAIT!
SIMPLICITY ITSELF!
TWO MEXICANS COOKING PANCAKES!
THIS TIME, I'LL CATCH YOU OUT, DUCOBOO!...
LIKE THE EXPERIENCED HARE, I SHALL WRIGGLE FREE FROM YOUR SNARE, MISS POACHER!
WHO'S THIS?
ERM?...
TWO MEXICANS ON A SKATEBOARD?
TWO MEXICANS SLOW-DANCING?
TWO MEXICANS...! NO, REALLY, I DON'T KNOW!
ONE DUCOBOO COPYING HIS CLASSMATE!
PAH! DOESN'T EVEN LOOK LIKE ME! FIRST OF ALL, I'VE GOT BLUE EYES!

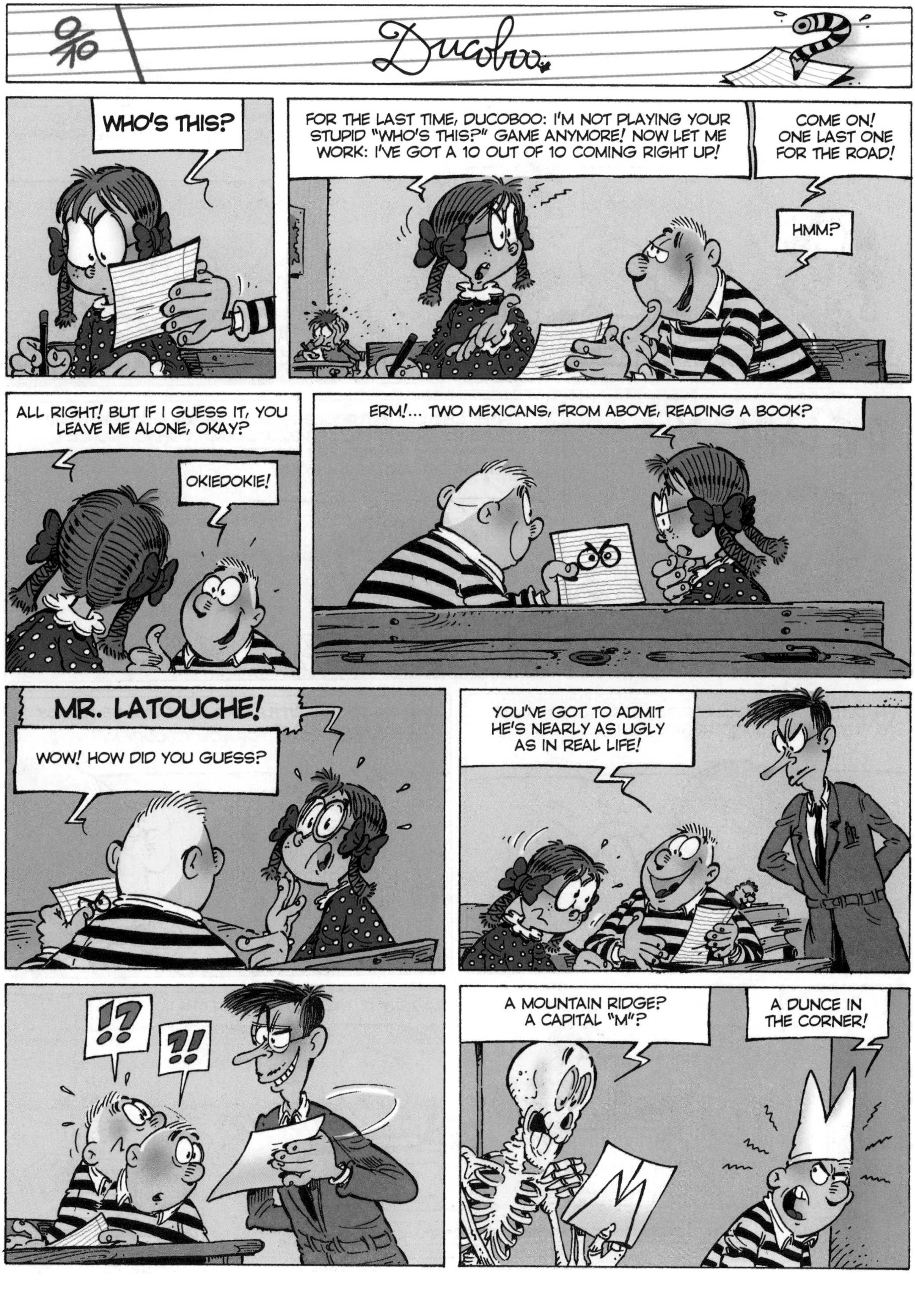
Ducoboo
WHO'S THIS?
FOR THE LAST TIME, DUCOBOO: I'M NOT PLAYING YOUR STUPID "WHO'S THIS?" GAME ANYMORE! NOW LET ME WORK: I'VE GOT A 10 OUT OF 10 COMING RIGHT UP!
COME ON! ONE LAST ONE FOR THE ROAD!
HMM?
ALL RIGHT! BUT IF I GUESS IT, YOU LEAVE ME ALONE, OKAY?
OKIEDOKIE!
ERM!... TWO MEXICANS, FROM ABOVE, READING A BOOK?
MR. LATOUCHE!
WOW! HOW DID YOU GUESS?
YOU'VE GOT TO ADMIT HE'S NEARLY AS UGLY AS IN REAL LIFE!
!?
?!
A MOUNTAIN RIDGE? A CAPITAL "M"?
A DUNCE IN THE CORNER!

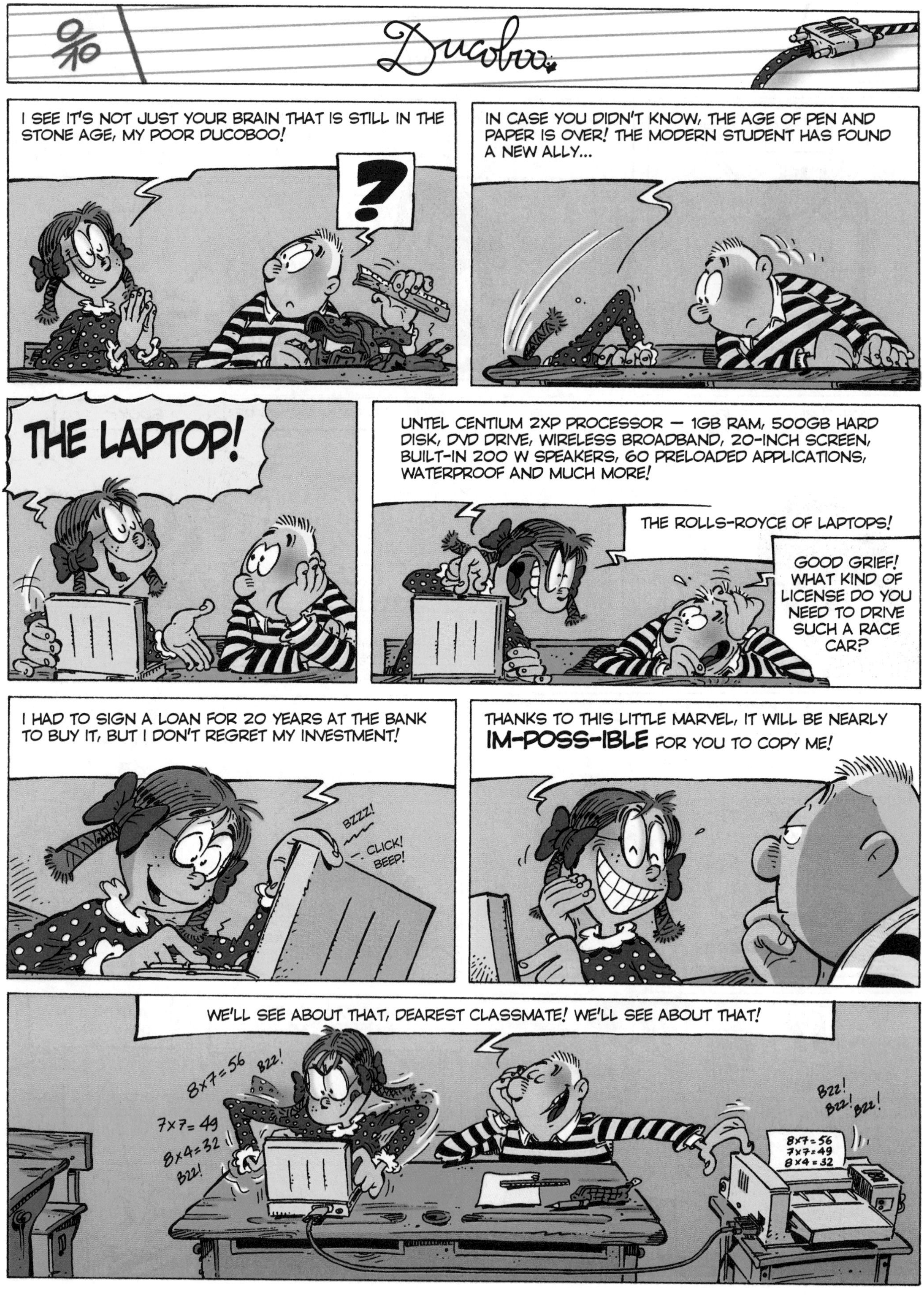
0/10
Ducoboo
I SEE IT'S NOT JUST YOUR BRAIN THAT IS STILL IN THE STONE AGE, MY POOR DUCOBOO!
?
IN CASE YOU DIDN'T KNOW, THE AGE OF PEN AND PAPER IS OVER! THE MODERN STUDENT HAS FOUND A NEW ALLY...
THE LAPTOP!
UNTEL CENTIUM 2XP PROCESSOR — 1GB RAM, 500GB HARD DISK, DVD DRIVE, WIRELESS BROADBAND, 20-INCH SCREEN, BUILT-IN 200 W SPEAKERS, 60 PRELOADED APPLICATIONS, WATERPROOF AND MUCH MORE!
THE ROLLS-ROYCE OF LAPTOPS!
GOOD GRIEF! WHAT KIND OF LICENSE DO YOU NEED TO DRIVE SUCH A RACE CAR?
I HAD TO SIGN A LOAN FOR 20 YEARS AT THE BANK TO BUY IT, BUT I DON'T REGRET MY INVESTMENT!
BZZZ!
CLICK!
BEEP!
THANKS TO THIS LITTLE MARVEL, IT WILL BE NEARLY **IM-POSS-IBLE** FOR YOU TO COPY ME!
WE'LL SEE ABOUT THAT, DEAREST CLASSMATE! WE'LL SEE ABOUT THAT!
8x7=56
BZZ!
7x7=49
8x4=32
BZZ!
BZZ!
BZZ!
BZZ!
8x7=56
7x7=49
8x4=32

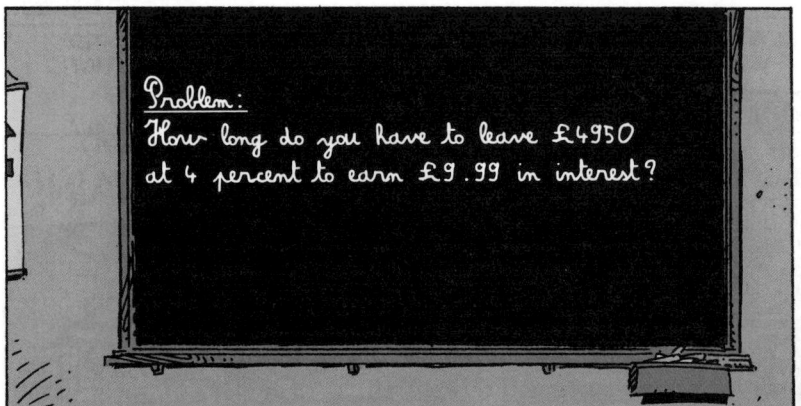

Problem:
How long do you have to leave £4950 at 4 percent to earn £9.99 in interest?

THIS IS IMPOSSIBLE: WHOEVER CAME UP WITH THIS PROBLEM MISSED HIS VOCATION AS A TORTURER!

I'LL TAKE THIS TIME, DUCOBOO, TO GIVE YOU A DEMONSTRATION OF THE MULTIPLE ADVANTAGES OF MY LAPTOP.

THIS GREAT MACHINE IS, IN FACT, LOADED WITH THE SOFTWARE "NO PROBLEMO H940."

IS IT ALSO LOADED WITH THE "VIRTUAL HUSBAND" SOFTWARE?

I INPUT THE DATA FOR THE PROBLEM...

TAP TAP! TAP TAP! TAP TAP!

I PUSH ENTER

AND THE MACHINE DOES THE REST!

NOW I JUST HAVE TO PRINT THE ANSWER AND THAT PRETTY 10 OUT OF 10 IS MINE!

BUT... WHAT... WHAT'S THIS?...

LOOKS LIKE A POWER CUT!

INDEED, JUST AT THE WRONG MOMENT, HERE COMES MR. LATOUCHE TO COLLECT THE PAPERS.

GULP!

BOOHOO!

BAH! DON'T WORRY: THE FIRST 0 OUT OF 10 HURTS THE MOST. BUT, YOU'LL SEE, YOU SOON GET USED TO IT!

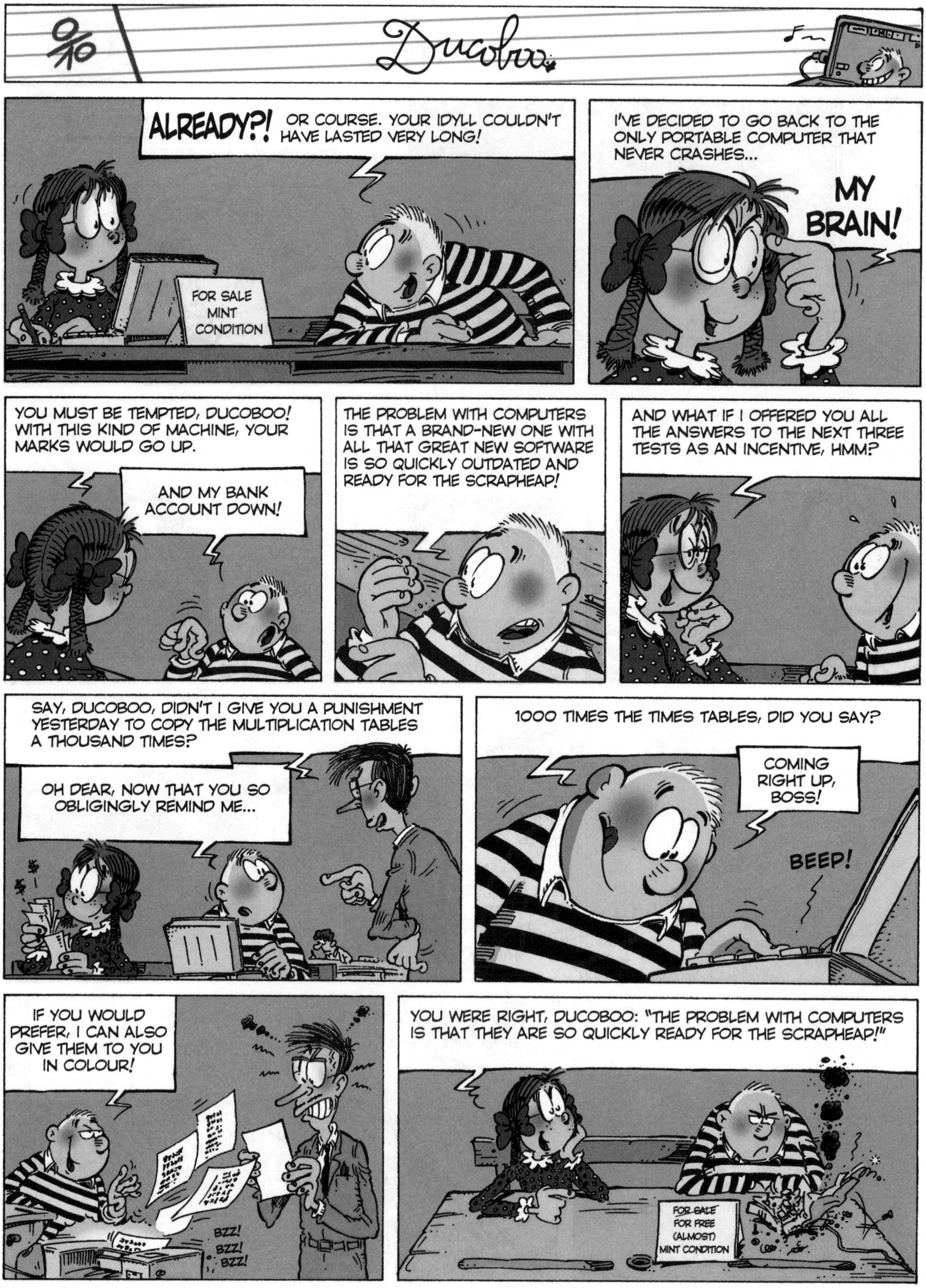

9/10
Ducoboo
ALREADY?!
OR COURSE. YOUR IDYLL COULDN'T HAVE LASTED VERY LONG!
FOR SALE MINT CONDITION
I'VE DECIDED TO GO BACK TO THE ONLY PORTABLE COMPUTER THAT NEVER CRASHES...
MY BRAIN!
YOU MUST BE TEMPTED, DUCOBOO! WITH THIS KIND OF MACHINE, YOUR MARKS WOULD GO UP.
AND MY BANK ACCOUNT DOWN!
THE PROBLEM WITH COMPUTERS IS THAT A BRAND-NEW ONE WITH ALL THAT GREAT NEW SOFTWARE IS SO QUICKLY OUTDATED AND READY FOR THE SCRAPHEAP!
AND WHAT IF I OFFERED YOU ALL THE ANSWERS TO THE NEXT THREE TESTS AS AN INCENTIVE, HMM?
SAY, DUCOBOO, DIDN'T I GIVE YOU A PUNISHMENT YESTERDAY TO COPY THE MULTIPLICATION TABLES A THOUSAND TIMES?
OH DEAR, NOW THAT YOU SO OBLIGINGLY REMIND ME...
1000 TIMES THE TIMES TABLES, DID YOU SAY?
COMING RIGHT UP, BOSS!
BEEP!
IF YOU WOULD PREFER, I CAN ALSO GIVE THEM TO YOU IN COLOUR!
BZZ!
BZZ!
BZZ!
YOU WERE RIGHT, DUCOBOO: "THE PROBLEM WITH COMPUTERS IS THAT THEY ARE SO QUICKLY READY FOR THE SCRAPHEAP!"
FOR SALE FOR FREE (ALMOST) MINT CONDITION

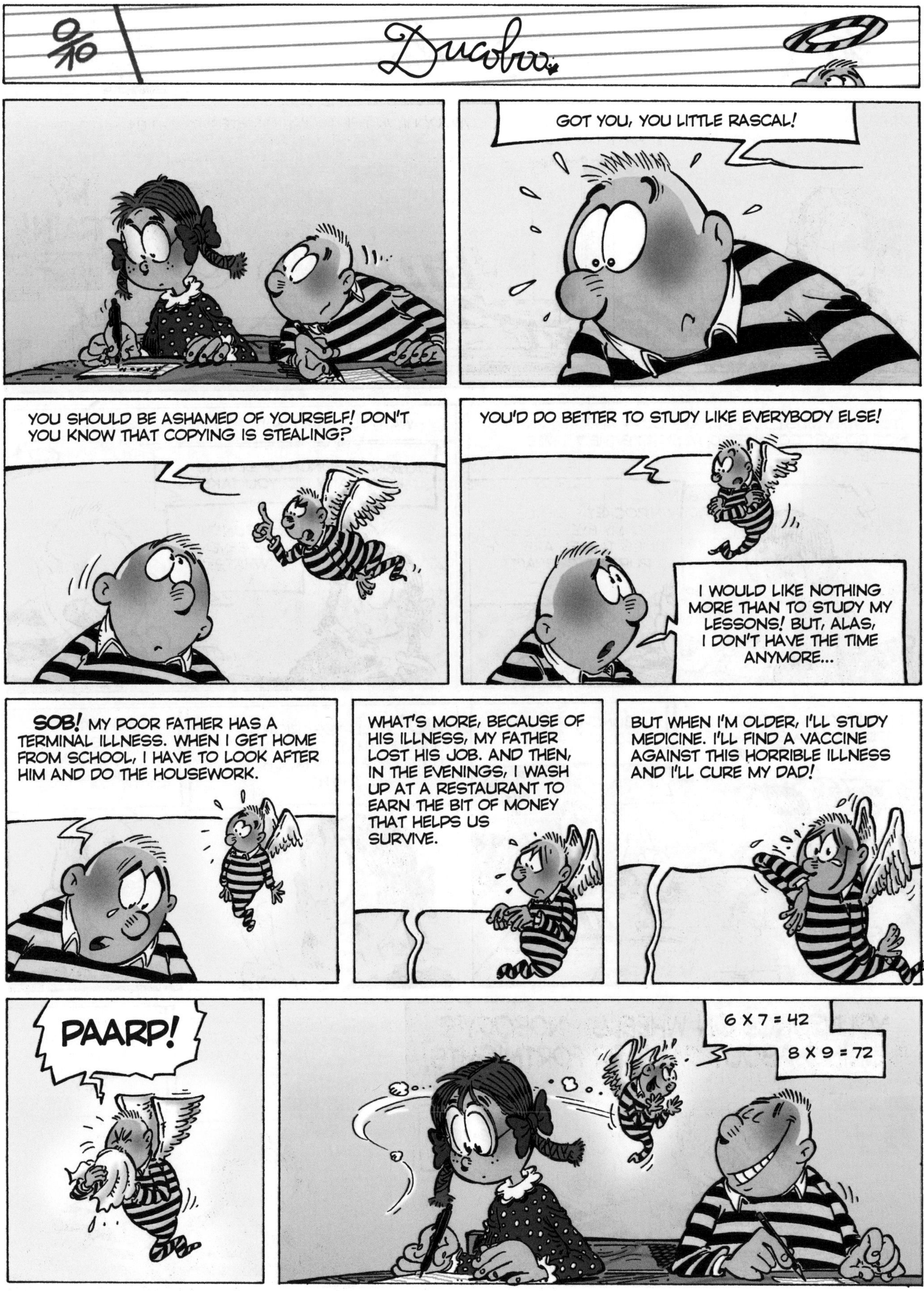
0/10
Ducobu
GOT YOU, YOU LITTLE RASCAL!
YOU SHOULD BE ASHAMED OF YOURSELF! DON'T YOU KNOW THAT COPYING IS STEALING?
YOU'D DO BETTER TO STUDY LIKE EVERYBODY ELSE!
I WOULD LIKE NOTHING MORE THAN TO STUDY MY LESSONS! BUT, ALAS, I DON'T HAVE THE TIME ANYMORE...
SOB! MY POOR FATHER HAS A TERMINAL ILLNESS. WHEN I GET HOME FROM SCHOOL, I HAVE TO LOOK AFTER HIM AND DO THE HOUSEWORK.
WHAT'S MORE, BECAUSE OF HIS ILLNESS, MY FATHER LOST HIS JOB. AND THEN, IN THE EVENINGS, I WASH UP AT A RESTAURANT TO EARN THE BIT OF MONEY THAT HELPS US SURVIVE.
BUT WHEN I'M OLDER, I'LL STUDY MEDICINE. I'LL FIND A VACCINE AGAINST THIS HORRIBLE ILLNESS AND I'LL CURE MY DAD!
PAARP!
6 X 7 = 42
8 X 9 = 72

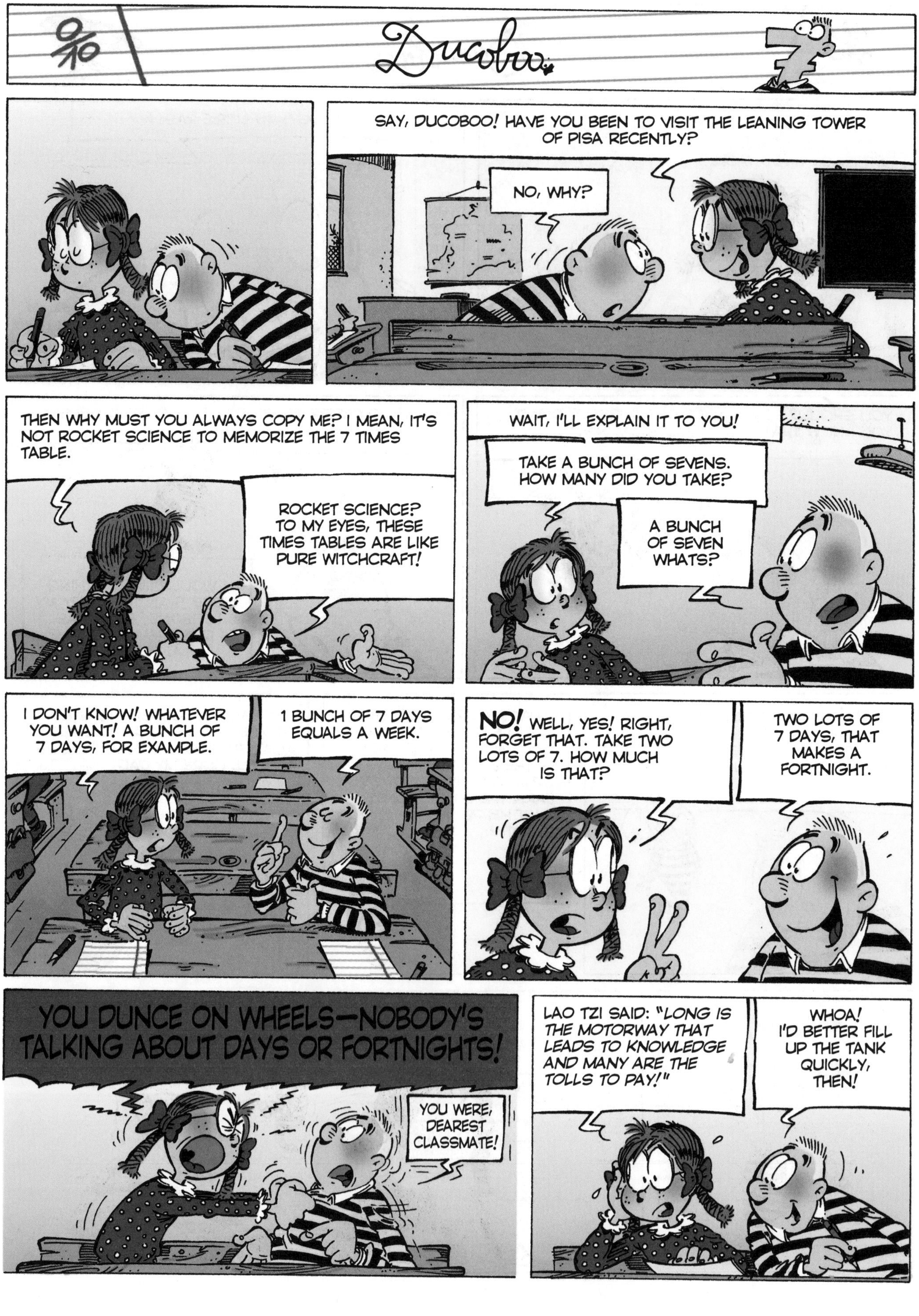
Ducoboo
0/10
SAY, DUCOBOO! HAVE YOU BEEN TO VISIT THE LEANING TOWER OF PISA RECENTLY?
NO, WHY?
THEN WHY MUST YOU ALWAYS COPY ME? I MEAN, IT'S NOT ROCKET SCIENCE TO MEMORIZE THE 7 TIMES TABLE.
ROCKET SCIENCE? TO MY EYES, THESE TIMES TABLES ARE LIKE PURE WITCHCRAFT!
WAIT, I'LL EXPLAIN IT TO YOU!
TAKE A BUNCH OF SEVENS. HOW MANY DID YOU TAKE?
A BUNCH OF SEVEN WHATS?
I DON'T KNOW! WHATEVER YOU WANT! A BUNCH OF 7 DAYS, FOR EXAMPLE.
1 BUNCH OF 7 DAYS EQUALS A WEEK.
NO! WELL, YES! RIGHT, FORGET THAT. TAKE TWO LOTS OF 7. HOW MUCH IS THAT?
TWO LOTS OF 7 DAYS, THAT MAKES A FORTNIGHT.
YOU DUNCE ON WHEELS—NOBODY'S TALKING ABOUT DAYS OR FORTNIGHTS!
YOU WERE, DEAREST CLASSMATE!
LAO TZI SAID: "LONG IS THE MOTORWAY THAT LEADS TO KNOWLEDGE AND MANY ARE THE TOLLS TO PAY!"
WHOA! I'D BETTER FILL UP THE TANK QUICKLY, THEN!

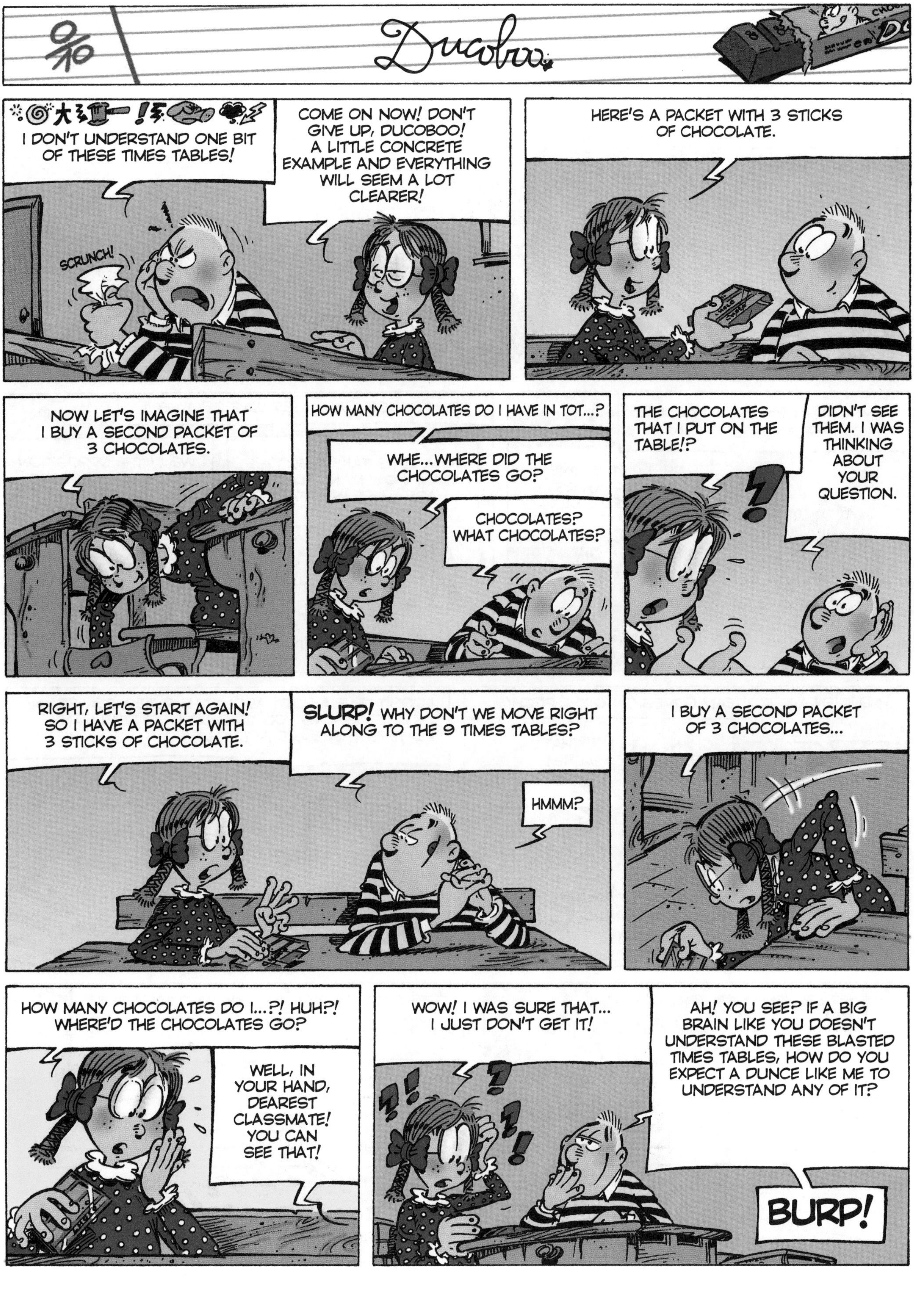

Ducoboo
I DON'T UNDERSTAND ONE BIT OF THESE TIMES TABLES!
SCRUNCH!
COME ON NOW! DON'T GIVE UP, DUCOBOO! A LITTLE CONCRETE EXAMPLE AND EVERYTHING WILL SEEM A LOT CLEARER!
HERE'S A PACKET WITH 3 STICKS OF CHOCOLATE.
NOW LET'S IMAGINE THAT I BUY A SECOND PACKET OF 3 CHOCOLATES.
HOW MANY CHOCOLATES DO I HAVE IN TOT...?
WHE...WHERE DID THE CHOCOLATES GO?
CHOCOLATES? WHAT CHOCOLATES?
THE CHOCOLATES THAT I PUT ON THE TABLE!?
DIDN'T SEE THEM. I WAS THINKING ABOUT YOUR QUESTION.
RIGHT, LET'S START AGAIN! SO I HAVE A PACKET WITH 3 STICKS OF CHOCOLATE.
SLURP! WHY DON'T WE MOVE RIGHT ALONG TO THE 9 TIMES TABLES?
HMMM?
I BUY A SECOND PACKET OF 3 CHOCOLATES...
HOW MANY CHOCOLATES DO I...?! HUH?! WHERE'D THE CHOCOLATES GO?
WELL, IN YOUR HAND, DEAREST CLASSMATE! YOU CAN SEE THAT!
WOW! I WAS SURE THAT... I JUST DON'T GET IT!
AH! YOU SEE? IF A BIG BRAIN LIKE YOU DOESN'T UNDERSTAND THESE BLASTED TIMES TABLES, HOW DO YOU EXPECT A DUNCE LIKE ME TO UNDERSTAND ANY OF IT?
BURP!

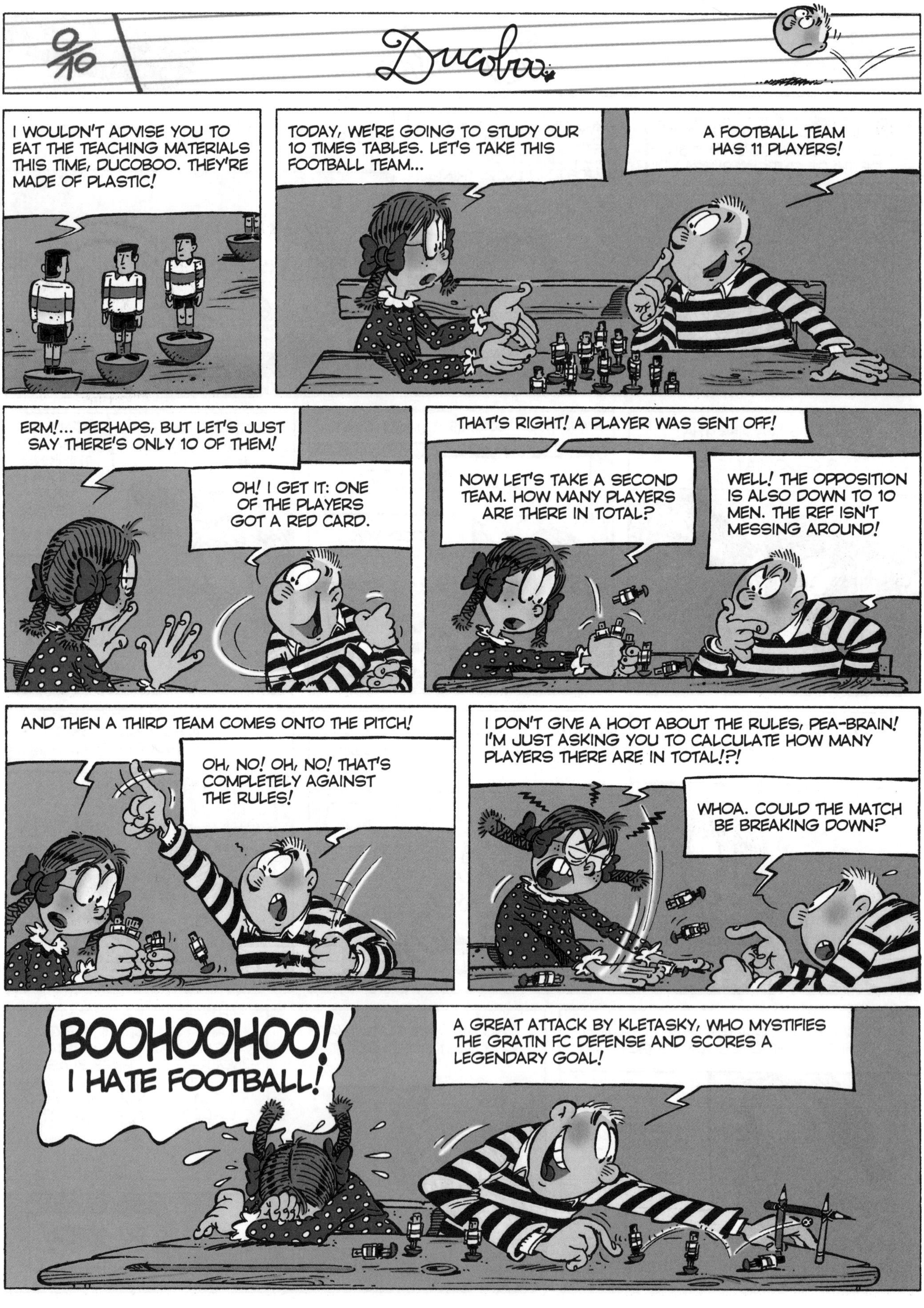
0/10
Ducoboo
I WOULDN'T ADVISE YOU TO EAT THE TEACHING MATERIALS THIS TIME, DUCOBOO. THEY'RE MADE OF PLASTIC!
TODAY, WE'RE GOING TO STUDY OUR 10 TIMES TABLES. LET'S TAKE THIS FOOTBALL TEAM...
A FOOTBALL TEAM HAS 11 PLAYERS!
ERM!... PERHAPS, BUT LET'S JUST SAY THERE'S ONLY 10 OF THEM!
OH! I GET IT: ONE OF THE PLAYERS GOT A RED CARD.
THAT'S RIGHT! A PLAYER WAS SENT OFF!
NOW LET'S TAKE A SECOND TEAM. HOW MANY PLAYERS ARE THERE IN TOTAL?
WELL! THE OPPOSITION IS ALSO DOWN TO 10 MEN. THE REF ISN'T MESSING AROUND!
AND THEN A THIRD TEAM COMES ONTO THE PITCH!
OH, NO! OH, NO! THAT'S COMPLETELY AGAINST THE RULES!
I DON'T GIVE A HOOT ABOUT THE RULES, PEA-BRAIN! I'M JUST ASKING YOU TO CALCULATE HOW MANY PLAYERS THERE ARE IN TOTAL!?!
WHOA. COULD THE MATCH BE BREAKING DOWN?
BOOHOOHOO! I HATE FOOTBALL!
A GREAT ATTACK BY KLETASKY, WHO MYSTIFIES THE GRATIN FC DEFENSE AND SCORES A LEGENDARY GOAL!

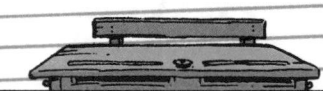

THANK YOU BOTH FOR ACCEPTING MY INVITATION. I THINK THAT IT'S TIME TO FIND A SOLUTION TO THE DISPUTE BETWEEN YOUR TWO CHILDREN...

I'VE GOT THE SOLUTION RIGHT HERE!

MAY I?

WITH THESE HORSE BLINKERS, THE CONFIDENTIALITY OF LEONIE'S WORK CAN NOW BE PRESERVED!

TAP! TAP! TAP! TAP!

ERM!... MR. DUCOBOO, WHAT DO YOU THINK OF THIS SOMEWHAT... BLINKERED IDEA?

MAY I?

THIS WAY, WITH THIS BIT BETWEEN THE TEETH, THE OLD MARE WON'T BITE ANYMORE!

RAAAH!

... LIVE FROM THE ST. SCHOLARUS RACECOURSE, WHERE BATTING GRATIN IN THE RED SPOTTED WHITE JERSEY, RIDING HER HIGH HORSE, IS RIGHT NOW CLOSING IN ON DUC O'BOO, IN THE YELLOW JERSEY WITH BLACK STRIPES!

Ducoboo

SANCTUS SCHOLARIUS ABBEY, JANUARY 1231.

ABBOT! ABBOT!

WHAT IS IT, SISTER LEONIE?

BROTHER DUCO WILLN'T STOP A-COPYING ME!

NAY, SAY I!

BROTHER DUCO! JUST BECAUSE THOU ART A COPYIST MONK DOESN'T MEANETH THAT THOU MUST COPY SISTER LEONIE!

FOR YOUR PENITENCE, THOU WILT SWIFTLY COPY OUT THESE THREE HEAVY TOMES!

BY JOVE! WHAT'S THIS?! NEVER HAVE I SEEN SUCH SINISTER FORMULAE!

7
1 × 7 = 7
2 × 7 = 14
3 × 7 = 21
× 7 = 28
7 = 35

8
1 × 8 = 8
2 × 8 = 16
3 × 8 = 24
4 × 8 = 32

HARK, MISCREANT, THIS HERE WAS HOW THE ARABIC MATHEMATICIANS WROTETH THEIR NUMBERS!

IT'S UNTO THEE THAT BEFALLETH THIS VERY NOBLE TASK OF TRANSFERRING THESE LEARNED WORKS CONTAINING MANY A MULTIPLICATION TO THE GENERATIONS TO COMETH!

PFFF! I CAN'T WAIT FOR THE INVENTION OF THE PRINTING PRESSETH!

AND THUS, BY CRUEL CHANCE, MY DISTANT ANCESTOR BECAME THE ONE THROUGH WHOM THOSE CURSED TIMES TABLES WERE PASSED DOWN TO US!

ANOTHER GREAT STORY, UNCLE DUCOBOO!

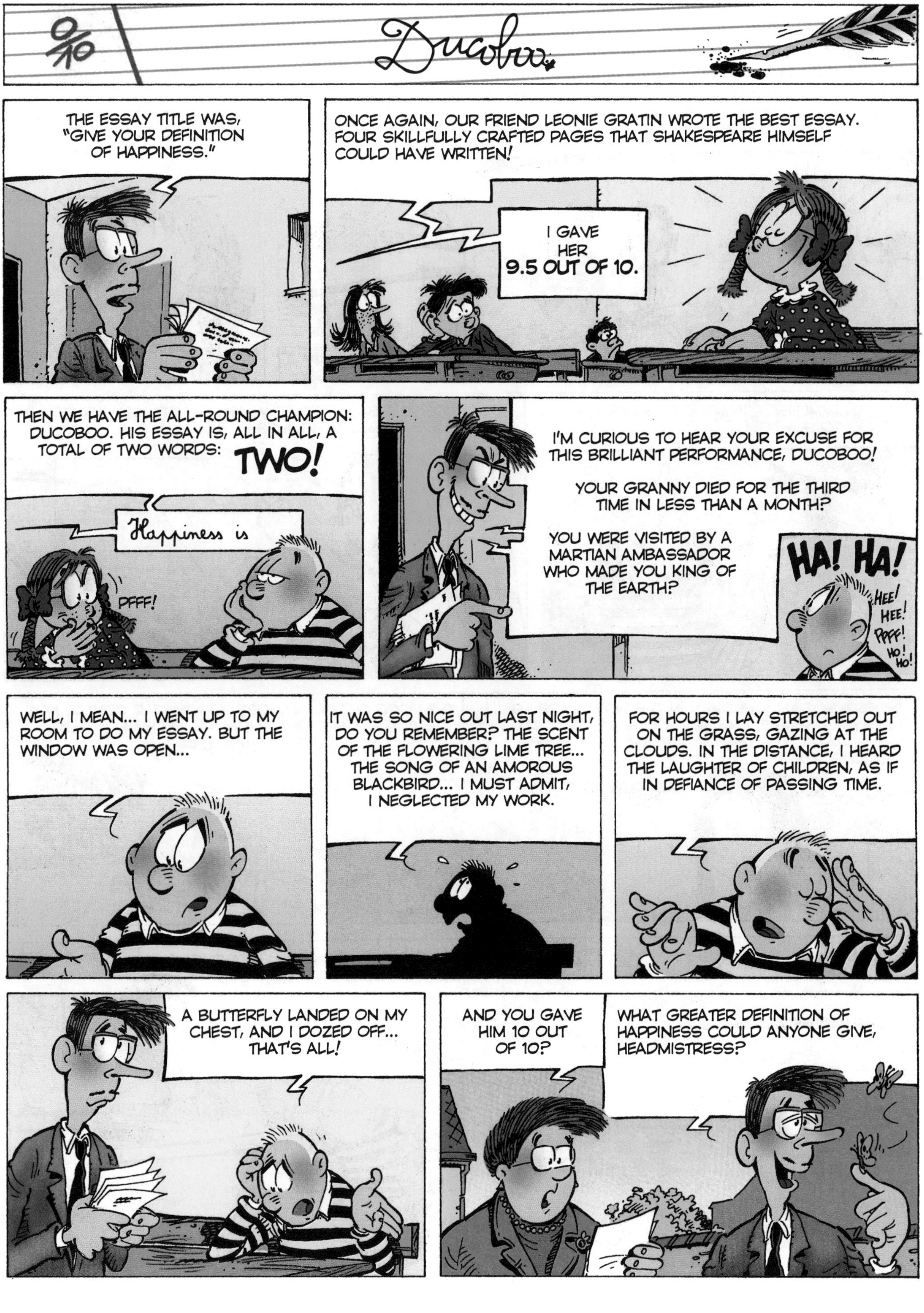
0/10
Ducoboo
THE ESSAY TITLE WAS, "GIVE YOUR DEFINITION OF HAPPINESS."
ONCE AGAIN, OUR FRIEND LEONIE GRATIN WROTE THE BEST ESSAY. FOUR SKILLFULLY CRAFTED PAGES THAT SHAKESPEARE HIMSELF COULD HAVE WRITTEN!
I GAVE HER 9.5 OUT OF 10.
THEN WE HAVE THE ALL-ROUND CHAMPION: DUCOBOO. HIS ESSAY IS, ALL IN ALL, A TOTAL OF TWO WORDS: TWO!
Happiness is
PFFF!
I'M CURIOUS TO HEAR YOUR EXCUSE FOR THIS BRILLIANT PERFORMANCE, DUCOBOO!
YOUR GRANNY DIED FOR THE THIRD TIME IN LESS THAN A MONTH?
YOU WERE VISITED BY A MARTIAN AMBASSADOR WHO MADE YOU KING OF THE EARTH?
HA! HA!
HEE! HEE! PPFF! HO! HO!
WELL, I MEAN... I WENT UP TO MY ROOM TO DO MY ESSAY. BUT THE WINDOW WAS OPEN...
IT WAS SO NICE OUT LAST NIGHT, DO YOU REMEMBER? THE SCENT OF THE FLOWERING LIME TREE... THE SONG OF AN AMOROUS BLACKBIRD... I MUST ADMIT, I NEGLECTED MY WORK.
FOR HOURS I LAY STRETCHED OUT ON THE GRASS, GAZING AT THE CLOUDS. IN THE DISTANCE, I HEARD THE LAUGHTER OF CHILDREN, AS IF IN DEFIANCE OF PASSING TIME.
A BUTTERFLY LANDED ON MY CHEST, AND I DOZED OFF... THAT'S ALL!
AND YOU GAVE HIM 10 OUT OF 10?
WHAT GREATER DEFINITION OF HAPPINESS COULD ANYONE GIVE, HEADMISTRESS?

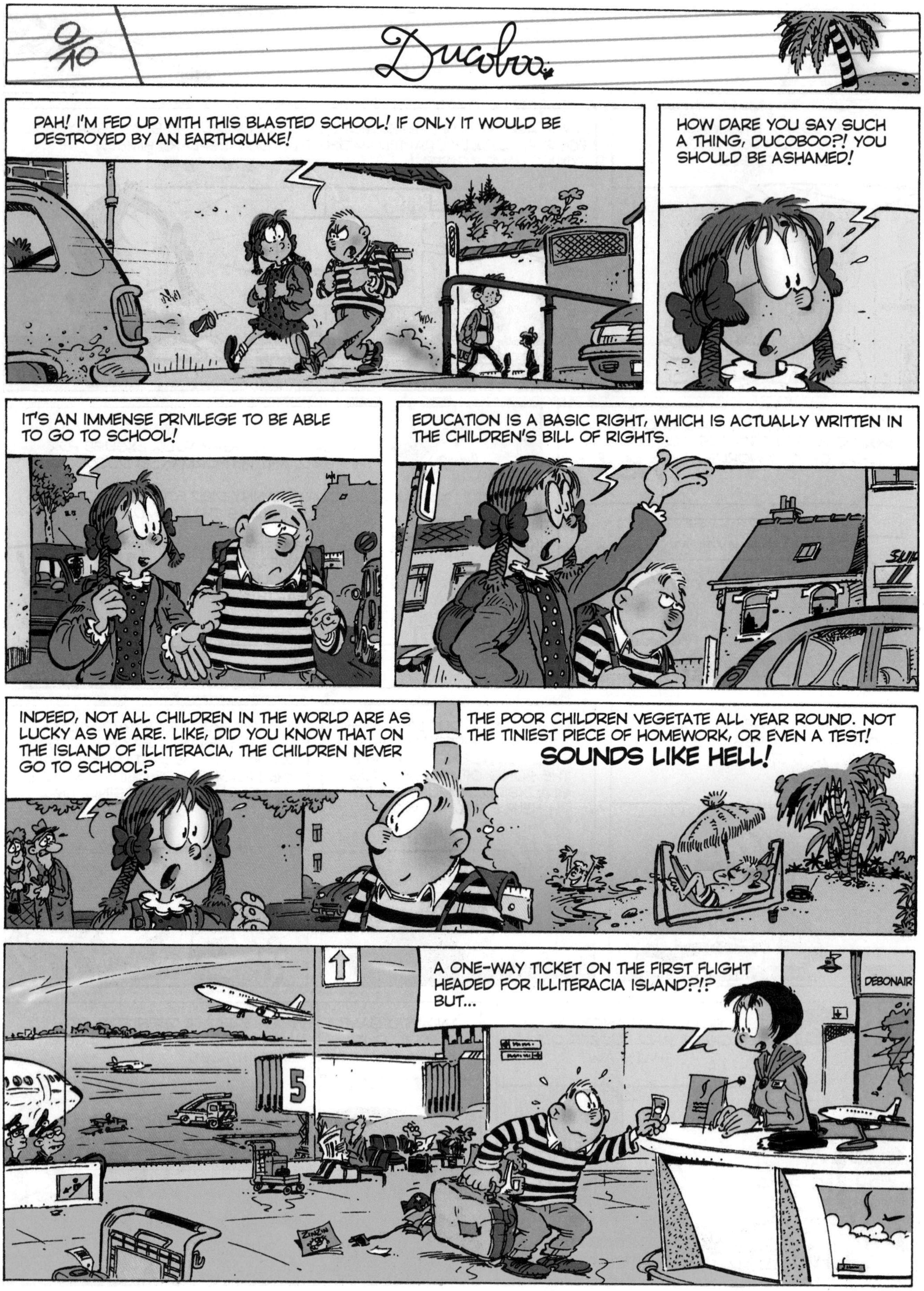
0/10
Ducoboo
PAH! I'M FED UP WITH THIS BLASTED SCHOOL! IF ONLY IT WOULD BE DESTROYED BY AN EARTHQUAKE!
HOW DARE YOU SAY SUCH A THING, DUCOBOO?! YOU SHOULD BE ASHAMED!
IT'S AN IMMENSE PRIVILEGE TO BE ABLE TO GO TO SCHOOL!
EDUCATION IS A BASIC RIGHT, WHICH IS ACTUALLY WRITTEN IN THE CHILDREN'S BILL OF RIGHTS.
INDEED, NOT ALL CHILDREN IN THE WORLD ARE AS LUCKY AS WE ARE. LIKE, DID YOU KNOW THAT ON THE ISLAND OF ILLITERACIA, THE CHILDREN NEVER GO TO SCHOOL?
THE POOR CHILDREN VEGETATE ALL YEAR ROUND. NOT THE TINIEST PIECE OF HOMEWORK, OR EVEN A TEST!
SOUNDS LIKE HELL!
A ONE-WAY TICKET ON THE FIRST FLIGHT HEADED FOR ILLITERACIA ISLAND?!? BUT...
DEBONAIR
5

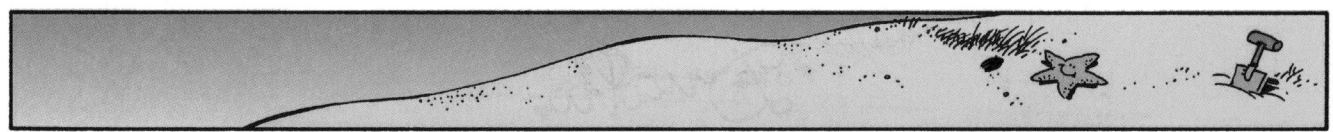

BEHAVIOUR: SMITH ||
DUCOBOO ||||| ||||| ||||| ||||| ||||| ||||| ||||| ||||| ||||| |

COME ON, GUSTAVE! GET A GRIP ON YOURSELF!

WE'RE ALL GOING ON A SUMMER HOLIDAY! NO MORE WORKING FOR A MONTH OR TWO...

MR. LATOUCHE?

I CAME TO WISH YOU A HAPPY HOLIDAY.

LEONIE GRATIN! HOW PROUD YOUR MOTHER MUST BE OF YOUR RESULTS!

FIRST IN THE CLASS WITH 99.9999%

I'M ESPECIALLY HAPPY THAT THE NASTY COPIER DUCOBOO WILL BE TAKING THE YEAR AGAIN.

NOW I CAN FINALLY BE RID OF THAT PARASITE!*

* THAT'S WHAT YOU THINK, LEONIE! (AN AUTHOR STICKING BY THE BREAD-WINNER'S SIDE)

DON'T RUB SALT IN THE WOUND! THINK ABOUT HAVING TO PUT UP WITH THAT DUNCE FOR ANOTHER WHOLE YEAR!

ERM... I... ER... THIS IS FOR YOU!

FOR ME?

SMOOCH!

SCRITCH! SCRITCH!

From the bottom of a little girl's heart, a great big thank you to my kind teacher,

Leonie Gratin

THERE, ANOTHER YEAR DONE! SEE YOU IN TWO MONTHS, BELOVED WORKPLACE!

CLICK CLACK!

I NEARLY FORGOT!

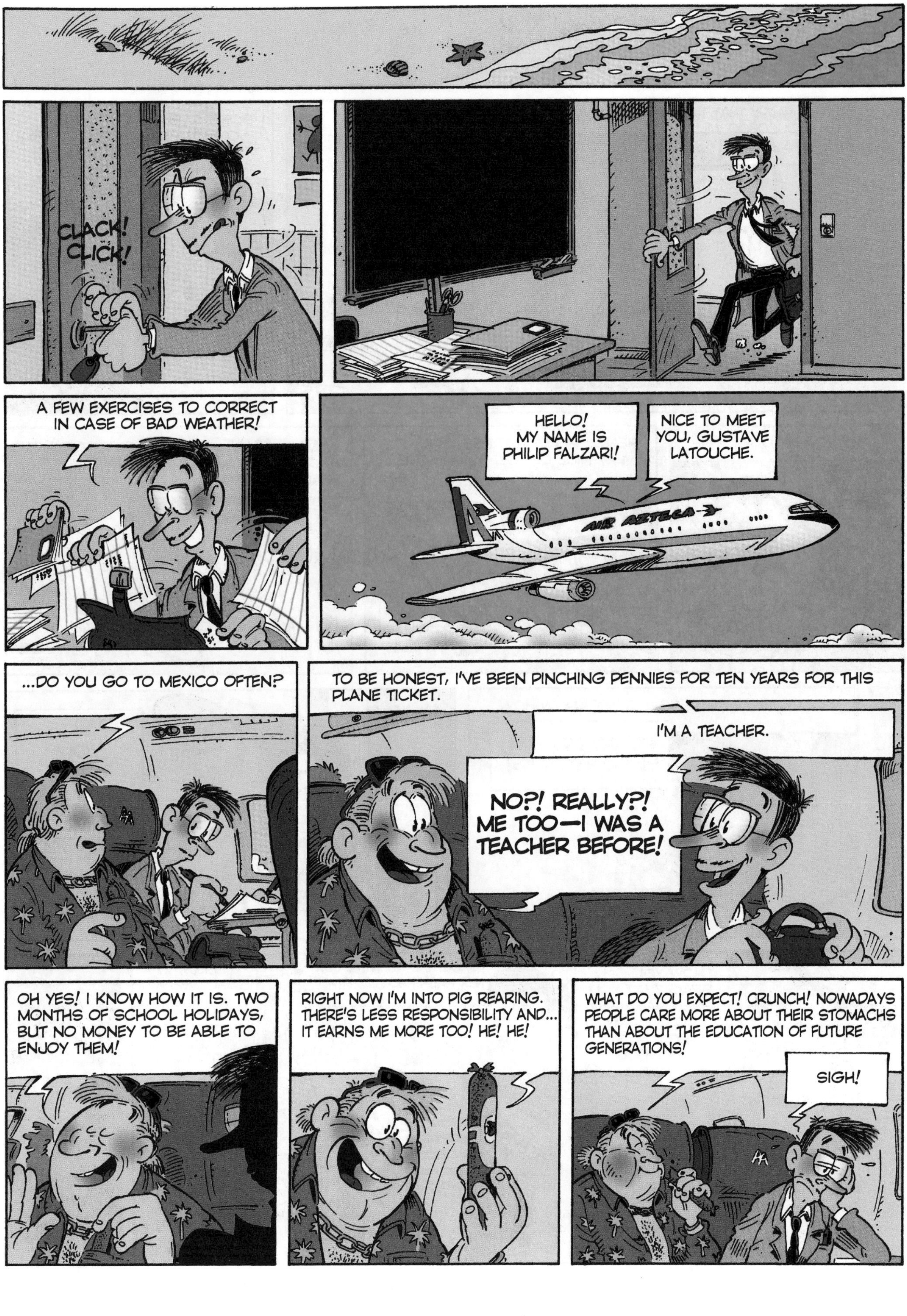
CLACK! CLICK!
A FEW EXERCISES TO CORRECT IN CASE OF BAD WEATHER!
HELLO! MY NAME IS PHILIP FALZARI!
NICE TO MEET YOU, GUSTAVE LATOUCHE.
AIR AZTECA
...DO YOU GO TO MEXICO OFTEN?
TO BE HONEST, I'VE BEEN PINCHING PENNIES FOR TEN YEARS FOR THIS PLANE TICKET.
I'M A TEACHER.
NO?! REALLY?! ME TOO—I WAS A TEACHER BEFORE!
OH YES! I KNOW HOW IT IS. TWO MONTHS OF SCHOOL HOLIDAYS, BUT NO MONEY TO BE ABLE TO ENJOY THEM!
RIGHT NOW I'M INTO PIG REARING. THERE'S LESS RESPONSIBILITY AND... IT EARNS ME MORE TOO! HE! HE!
WHAT DO YOU EXPECT! CRUNCH! NOWADAYS PEOPLE CARE MORE ABOUT THEIR STOMACHS THAN ABOUT THE EDUCATION OF FUTURE GENERATIONS!
SIGH!

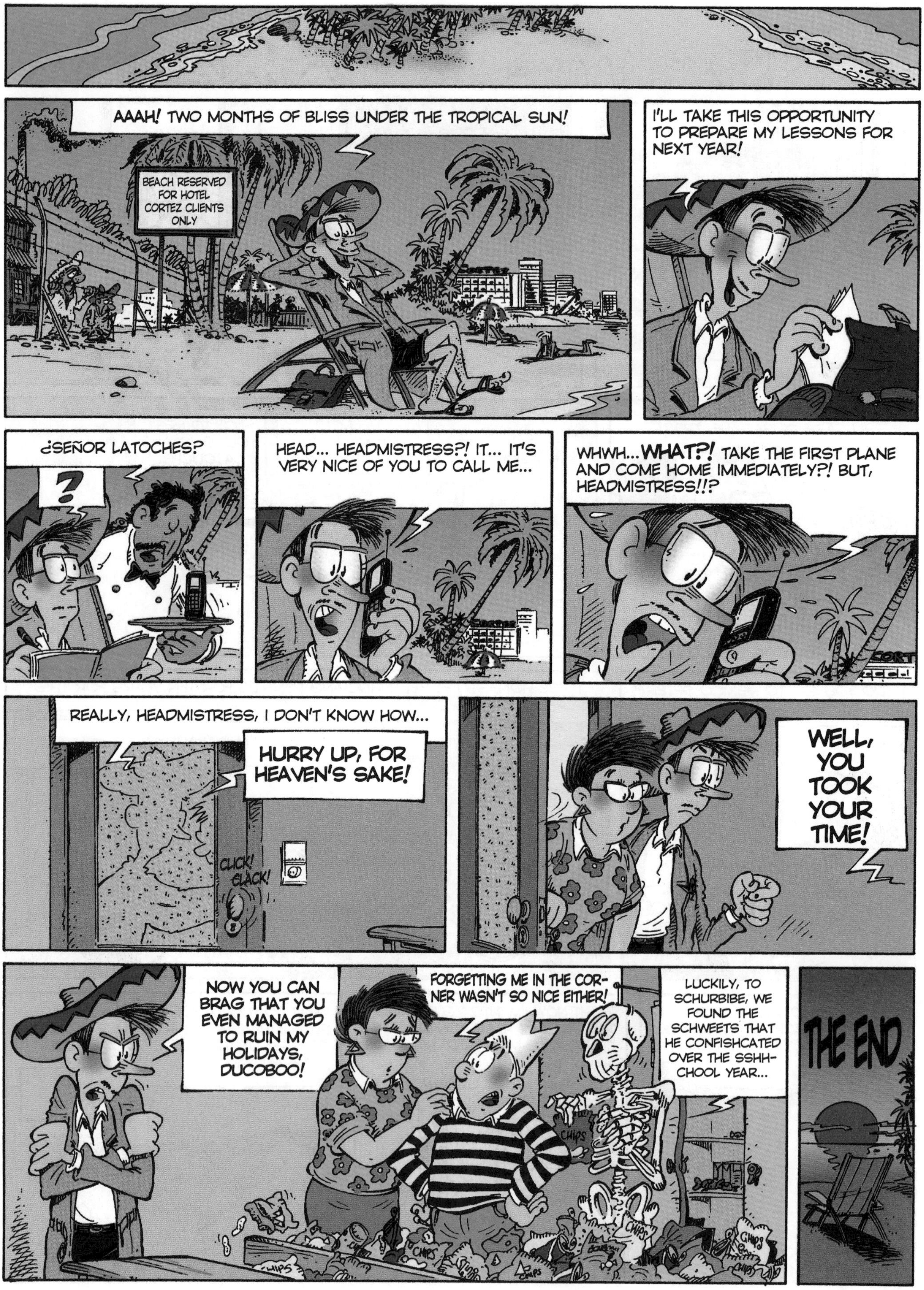
AAAH! TWO MONTHS OF BLISS UNDER THE TROPICAL SUN!
BEACH RESERVED FOR HOTEL CORTEZ CLIENTS ONLY
I'LL TAKE THIS OPPORTUNITY TO PREPARE MY LESSONS FOR NEXT YEAR!
¿SEÑOR LATOCHES?
?
HEAD... HEADMISTRESS?! IT... IT'S VERY NICE OF YOU TO CALL ME...
WHWH...WHAT?! TAKE THE FIRST PLANE AND COME HOME IMMEDIATELY?! BUT, HEADMISTRESS!!?
REALLY, HEADMISTRESS, I DON'T KNOW HOW...
HURRY UP, FOR HEAVEN'S SAKE!
CLICK! CLACK!
WELL, YOU TOOK YOUR TIME!
NOW YOU CAN BRAG THAT YOU EVEN MANAGED TO RUIN MY HOLIDAYS, DUCOBOO!
FORGETTING ME IN THE CORNER WASN'T SO NICE EITHER!
LUCKILY, TO SCHURBIBE, WE FOUND THE SCHWEETS THAT HE CONFISHCATED OVER THE SSHH-CHOOL YEAR...
THE END

Godi + Zidrou
1
Ducoboo
King of the Dunces
CINEBOOK The 9th Art Publisher

1 - King of the Dunces

Godi + Zidrou
2
Ducoboo
In the corner!
CINEBOOK The 9th Art Publisher

2 - In the Corner!

Godi + Zidrou
3
Ducoboo
Your answers or your life!
CINEBOOK The 9th Art Publisher

3 - Your Answers or Your Life!

9th CINEBOOK
The 9th Art Publisher
www.cinebook.com

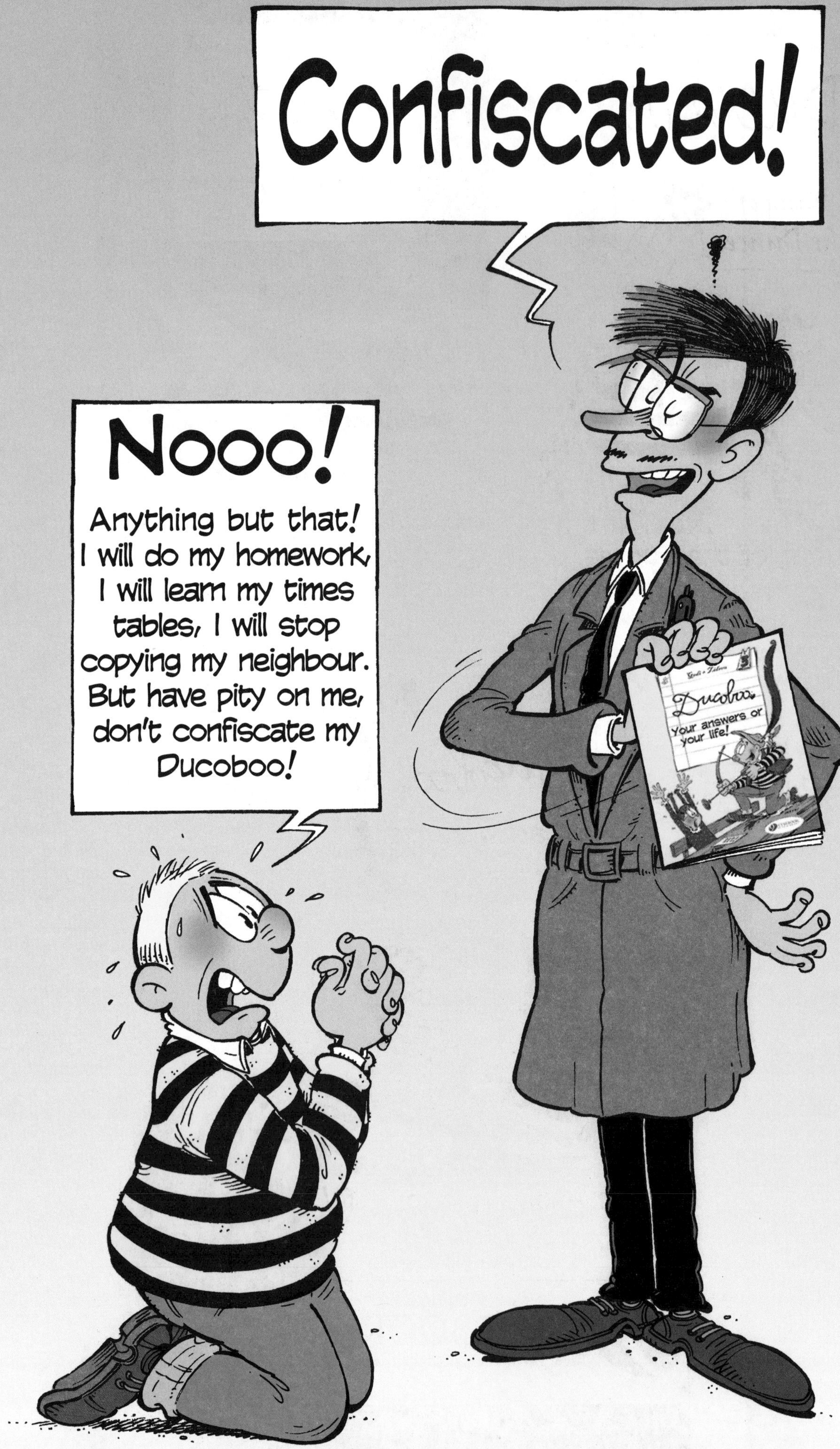
Confiscated!
Nooo!
Anything but that! I will do my homework, I will learn my times tables, I will stop copying my neighbour. But have pity on me, don't confiscate my Ducoboo!
Ducoboo
Your answers or your life!